A Passion for Cultural Studies

University of the
West of England

BRISTOL

Also by Ben Highmore:

Michel de Certeau: Analysing culture

Cityscapes: Cultural readings in the material and symbolic city

Everyday Life and Cultural Theory: An introduction

The Design Culture Reader

The Everyday Life Reader

A Passion for Cultural Studies

BEN HIGHMORE

Reader in Media and Cultural Studies, University of Sussex, UK

palgrave
macmillan

© Ben Highmore 2009

First published 2009 by
PALGRAVE MACMILLAN

Palgrave Macmillan in the UK is an imprint of Macmillan Publishers Limited,
registered in England, company number 785998, of Houndmills, Basingstoke, Hampshire
RG21 6XS.

Palgrave Macmillan in the US is a division of St Martin's Press LLC,
175 Fifth Avenue, New York, NY 10010.

Palgrave Macmillan is the global academic imprint of the above companies
and has companies and representatives throughout the world.

Palgrave® and Macmillan® are registered trademarks in the United States, the United
Kingdom, Europe and other countries.

ISBN-13: 978–1–4039–9717–3   hardback
ISBN-10: 1–4039–9717–9   hardback
ISBN-13: 978–1–4039–9718–0   paperback
ISBN-10: 1–4039–9718–7   paperback

This book is printed on paper suitable for recycling and made from fully
managed and sustained forest sources. Logging, pulping and manufacturing processes
are expected to conform to the environmental regulations of the country of origin.

A catalogue record for this book is available from the British Library.

A catalog record for this book is available from the Library of Congress.

10   9   8   7   6   5   4   3   2   1
18 17 16 15 14 13 12 11 10 09

Printed and bound in Great Britain by
CPI Antony Rowe, Chippenham and Eastbourne

To see ourselves as others see us can be eye-opening. To see others as sharing a nature with ourselves is the merest decency. But it is from the far more difficult achievement of seeing ourselves amongst others, as a local example of the forms human life has locally taken, a case among cases, a world among worlds, that the largeness of mind, without which objectivity is self-congratulation and tolerance a sham, comes.

(Geertz 1993: 16)

Contents

List of Figures

Preface and Acknowledgements

This book is intended to do two things. First, it is designed to introduce the field of cultural studies to both the initiated and the uninitiated through a series of sketches of various cultural phenomena (commodities, communication, and so on). My proposition is simple: culture is animated; it is driven by forces, forces that I will call 'passions'. Of course culture consists of meanings and ideas, but meanings are insignificant if they don't take hold and bite, if they don't circulate with energy. To believe that the world is flat, for example, is simply an opinion, a meaning attached to the world. To vociferously defend the flatness of the world and to denounce world-roundedness, and those who believe in world-roundedness, is to enter a world of cultural passion. This is the form of culture that matters.

The second intention for this book is more tentative. I want this book to instil a passion for cultural studies in you the reader and, perhaps most especially, in readers new to cultural studies. The proof of that particular pudding will be in the eating, of course. What I didn't want to do, though, was to offer a definition of cultural studies, or give you a history of its institutional life, a catalogue of its achievements and mistakes, its successes and failures. Cultural studies is a permission slip to work across disciplines and to explore diverse phenomena; to look for a coherent set of approaches and practices within it would be to miss out on its most seductive charms. Much better, I felt, would be to plunge straight in to the messy business of culture, to dirty my hands (and yours) on the rough and clammy textures of experience. Rather than try to persuade you about the correctness of an interpretation, I want to show you cultural passions as they circulate, coalesce, and resonate.

The showing that I propose here is historical and cross-cultural. The path I take is necessarily picaresque and fragmented. I want to cover as much ground as possible in this short introductory volume. In a sense then this is a collage of snapshots designed to demonstrate cultural studies' reach and range: an inventory, of sorts, of the kinds of interests that cultural studies has and can pursue. I look at media and migration, commodities and conflict: there are jump cuts, abrupt changes in cultural tone, moments of exuberance followed quickly by scenes of cultural violence. What links these snapshots is an orientation towards passion; towards the affects and feelings that culture invokes and provokes.

If culture is, most often, the field of 'second nature', where the most intimate and ordinary aspects of life often appear as 'common sense', then one of the central tasks of the study of culture is to show these aspects as 'local' examples, as 'a case among cases', rather than as universal practices that other 'cultures' deviate from. From this perspective there is no cultural deviation: or rather, all is deviation, all diversity. To look across cultures (both historically and geographically) should alter our 'own' proximal culture. I don't know where you are from, or where you are now, I don't know your sexual preferences, your animating enthusiasms, your beliefs, your social and ethical affiliations, or your politics. I don't know if you're reading this to help write a term paper, or out of general interest; you may be sitting near a computer in rural Canada, or in a busy library in Beijing. Your first language may or may not be English. Your skin may or may not be dark; your passport may hinder your movement around the globe or allow you freedom of movement. Your religious affiliations may cause anxiety to some; your lack of religious faith provoking bemusement in others. Proximal culture – that sense of what is culturally near and distant, intimate and foreign, common or strange – is always a local matter. But to see it as a local matter also (and necessarily) means looking elsewhere.

To see proximal culture as local, as only one way of doing things, can have unnerving effects. To see your own, most intimately held beliefs as local custom can be to estrange yourself from them. Sometimes, though, I think that this is almost impossible to do in any real meaningful way. The chances of simply being able to recognise your own customs of hygiene, for instance, or eating as locally specific, and no different in value from practices you have learnt to see as dirty or impolite, may be something that is much more easily argued than passionately lived. It might take years before a cultural form that you grew up with can reveal itself as strangely local (it is only recently that the Christian religion has become truly cultish and strange for me, rather than the dull backdrop of childhood). This book argues that while such estrangements are useful, they too have their own passionate affects. Estrangement, anxiety, embarrassment, disorientation are passionate forms just as much as ardour, enthusiasm, attachment and love. It is a task of this book to take the term 'passion' away from those who would seek to see passion as simply a 'good thing'.

I get the feeling that the most common use of the term passion is as a synonym for enthusiasm. For example you might be told that 'to get this job you must be passionate about food', or that 'passion is much more important than experience'. (Usually when people are telling you how important passion is for a job they are subtly letting you know that there won't be much money in it.) Yet passion, especially historically, has been associated as much with suffering and emotional pain as with zeal and eagerness. Indeed the links between the two become much clearer as soon as you imagine a passion or desire that fails to reach its goal. It only hurts because you care so much. A refugee's passionate pain for their homeland is obviously connected to their emotional attachment to a place of belonging. Intense amorous passion can be accompanied by the pain (imagined, anticipated) of loss and rejection. This is all part of culture, its animating energy, but it is also (I think) part of the animating energy of studying culture, or studying culture in a way that matters, in a way that matters to you. I hope, here, that pleasure (or something like it) might at least give the pain a run for its money.

This book is dedicated to all those who have made me, and kept me, passionate about cultural studies. The specific impetus came from talking to Catherine Gray, the book's initial editor at Palgrave, about different ways of conceiving an introduction to cultural studies. Emily Salz, the book's subsequent editor, has been characteristically patient, generous and supportive. The writing of the book was delayed slightly when I moved institutions, but now, here at the University of Sussex (my current academic home) I have found excellent new colleagues who are passionate about cultural studies. Before moving to Sussex I spend thirteen happy years at the University of the West of England, Bristol and looking back I realise that it provided a truly accommodating environment for cultural studies.

The author and the publishers would like to thank the following for their kind permission to reproduce copyright material: the author and Methuen Drama, an imprint of A&C Black Publishers

Ltd, for the quotation from Stephen Poliakoff's *Shooting the Past*; Paul Grendon for the use of his photograph 'District Six Museum interior 2007', reproduced also with kind permission of the District Six Museum; Kevin Roche John Dinkeloo and Associates for the photograph of the IBM Pavilion at the New York World's Fair 1964–5; T-Mobile and Rebecca Blond Associates for the still from T-Mobile Flext advert (2008); The Art Archive and Culver Pictures for the use of 'His Master's Voice' – an early advertisement for RCA Victor; Susan Hiller for the use of 'Belshazzar's Feast', reproduced also with kind permission of Timothy Taylor Gallery, London.

Every effort has been made to trace all the copyright holders, but if any have been inadvertently overlooked the publisher will be pleased to make the necessary arrangement at the first opportunity.

1 Introduction – Passionate Culture

In this chapter, after briefly examining the current usage of the term passion, I want to show the importance of the passions for the study of culture. Since classical times through to the enlightenment, the term 'the passions' was used to designate what later thinkers called emotions, or affects, or aesthetic life (the life that wasn't governed by rationality). One way of characterising cultural studies would be to see it as an inquiry into passionate culture (culture caught in the highs and lows of life, culture-in-process).

These days 'passion' is a hot ingredient used to spice up advertising campaigns. A clothing company is 'fuelled by passion'; this manufacturer of pasta sauces is 'passionate about food'. A recent advertising campaign designed to promote the North East of England claims that the whole area is 'passionate about business', and just in case you hadn't realised quite how passionate the North East is, the advert ran a tag line stating 'passionate people, passionate places: North East England' (*Guardian Weekend* 8 August 2007). And it is not just advertising that is passionate about passion, other forms of promotional culture are in on the act too: TV chefs such as Gordon Ramsay go around the UK and the US berating the cooks of underachieving restaurants for just not being passionate enough. Gordon Ramsay's career is built on mobilising 'passion': his first book was titled *Gordon Ramsay's Passion for Flavour* and his manner as a TV presenter is of someone who is just so irrepressibly passionate that he is simply jumping up and down with excitement.

Passion is also a favourite these days with writers of self-help literature. The motivational writer (and speaker) Mark Sanborn encourages his readers to go that 'extra mile' in their work so that they can find fulfilment in their lives while also improving the lives of others. His book is named after 'a mail carrier who passionately loves his job and who genuinely cares about the people he serves' (Sanborn 2004: back cover). The book is called *The Fred Factor: How passion*

in your work and life can turn the ordinary into the extraordinary.
Passion here is the currency of the service sector (the book is filled
with airline stewards, hotel staff and waiters), where 'adding
value' through personal service, is the way a company might find
a competitive edge. In *The Fred Factor* passion is never oriented
towards struggling for better conditions by joining a union, nor is
'passion' (in the shape of anger, or shame) something that might
result from the way that you are treated by customers and bosses
within a service industry trying to squeeze more (poorly-remuner-
ated) work out of you. Passion is, here, an acceptance of the order
of things and desire to make the 'best' of it.

Janet Bray Attwood and Chris Attwood (a former married couple
who are now partners in an advice business) mix an *ad hoc* religious sensibility with instrumental business get-go. *The Passion
Test: The Effortless Path to Discovering Your Destiny*, is a sort of
new-age, performance-enhancing, caring, outward-looking guide
to having everything (money, great relationships and spiritual
well-being). The online magazine the two founded sum it up perfectly: 'Healthy Wealthy nWise'. The book also includes within it
a constant stream of endorsements from others (*The Passion Test*
changed my life, so you must read it) to the point where the whole
thing reads like an advert for itself. One endorsement is from a
man who is a specialist in 'turning corporate underperformers into
marketing and sales whizzes' (Attwood and Attwood 2007: 174).
And of course the magic ingredient is always passion. Just be passionate; just do it. The sense of self-serving profiteering seems to
mark everything: open yourself up to friends (you never know
how useful they can be), make time for your lover (you don't want
to go without sex), find something special about yourself (and sell
it to everyone).

But passion hasn't always meant unbridled enthusiasm; nor has it
always highlighted romantic love as the pinnacle of passion. What
these two senses of the term do get right (and what links these
everyday meanings to an older sense of the term passion) is the
connection between passion and energy. In an earlier time passion
was the varied qualities of energy that arose in relation to our
communion with the world, with each other. René Descartes, writing in the 1640s enumerated the passions as: wonder, esteem,
scorn, generosity, pride, humility, servility, veneration, disdain,

love, hatred, desire, hope, apprehension, jealousy, confidence, despair, irresolution, courage, boldness, emulation, cowardice, terror, remorse, joy, sadness, mockery, envy, pity, self-satisfaction, repentance, approval, gratitude, indignation, anger, vainglory, shame, distaste, regret, and lightheartedness (Descartes 1989 [1649]: 52–55). Passion is about the pull and push of your connection to the social world, it is about the ebbs and flows of your feelings, the peaks and troughs of your liveliness, the pounding of your creaturely-ness. Descartes' list is obviously more expansive, more nuanced, than the meanings that currently circulate with the term passion. It is, for this reason alone, infinitely more useful for locating the forms and objects of attention that are central to this book.

The simple purpose of this book, and its modest argument, is to generate a passionate enthusiasm (an enthusiasm that would be modulated through anger, apprehension, and many of the other passions on Descartes' list) by exploring culture as a passionate field. Passionate culture, in this book, includes the passions as they existed for enlightenment philosophers, as well as what they become when people started talking about emotions and affects instead. As well as passions and emotions I want to include, in my store cupboard of possibilities, moods and feelings more generally. So while anger and fear might be thought of as 'vehement passions', there are a host of other arenas of passionate culture that don't rely on vehemence (a sudden intense experience) but have a more diffused intensity. Irritation, nostalgia, the feeling of the uncanny, homesickness, boredom – such 'minor affects' (Ngai 2005: 354) – don't necessarily take hold of you in a split second; they creep up on you, like a slow uncomfortable ache.

In 1884 the philosopher and psychologist William James described the mind's aesthetic sphere as 'its longings, its pleasures and pains and its emotions' (James 1884: 188). This opening-out of the term aesthetic (which can often be reduced to discussion of art and beauty) is similar to the opening-out I want to allow for the term passion. The word 'feeling' also has that varied sense of physicality, energy, and state of mind. To see this realm of experience and materiality as central to the study of culture is, I think, crucial, especially when we consider the particularity of what is meant by the term culture. One useful definition of culture is offered by Steven Connor:

> I think that what we mean by a culture is a collectivity with an inside. To refer to an organised set of social habits, behaviours and relations as a culture is to see those habits, behaviours and relations as expressive rather than merely characteristic. Your culture is what you are, rather than what you do. So when one is speaking of a culture, one is scooping out a space for an imagined subject of that culture, and construing it therefore as a collective form of consciousness and feeling.
>
> (Connor 2003: non-paginated)

Culture is, as we will see throughout this book, intimately connected to feelings. And it is the sense of intimacy that is crucial too: culture is the social as it is intimately experienced; at it moves from 'out there' to 'in here' – or at least to 'near here'.

The question of the interiority of passionate culture is worth debating. Do my feelings bubble-up from within, so to speak, or do they circulate around me, enlivening my world, extending me outwards in my connections and disconnections with others? Most of the time my emotions feel like they come from within (the rhythms of my heart might tell me this) but when I cry in response to a particularly sentimental film, for instance, aren't I 'catching' a passionate energy from 'out there'? Passionate culture, then, might most usefully be seen as the way cultural passions catch hold of us, attach us to ideas and beliefs, and in doing so 'scoop' out a space for an imagined subject of that culture.

For some this orientation towards feelings will be a signal that we are entering a territory of vagueness and insubstantiality. As I'm writing this the news is constantly telling me that the global economy is imploding, banks are going bankrupt, businesses are loosing billions of dollars and euros, not to mention the woes of those with 'toxic' mortgages. The reason, we are told, is 'loss of confidence'. The corporate whizzes, that an arm of the passion industry is dedicated to, are generating a different kind of passion now. Trepidation has stolen the stage from reckless enthusiasm. And this passion of uncertainty and anxiety is contagious; it grows as it moves from country to country, piling up financial nervousness on economic doubt. It seems as if the whole structure of international finance was propped up on that most insubstantial of things – 'faith'. Or rather, perhaps it is now time to see the substance, the materiality, and the large-scale cultural affects of passion.

This book doesn't attempt to deal with the passions systematically or exhaustively (in the further reading I suggest a range of books that explore that dimension of passionate culture). Many passions, emotions and moods are ignored. This is not the point of the book. Mine is an invitation to the realm of studying culture, and for starting out with the matters that matter, the passionate matters. Here I want to paint with a broad brush, to pick vivid moments of passionate culture as they link up to some of the central preoccupations of cultural studies (commodity culture, the media, migration, identity, and so on): passion is a starting point rather than a goal in itself. But while the careful articulation of the passions is not this book's destination, it is worth spending some words looking at the provenance of this term and how it has been used.

THINGS THAT QUICKEN THE HEART

In common English usage the words designating passionate experience sit awkwardly on the borders of the material and the immaterial, the physical and metaphysical: we are *moved* by a sentiment; our *feelings* are hurt; I am *touched* by your generosity. The interlacing of sensual, physical experience (here, the insistent reference to the haptic realm – touch, feel, move) with the passionate intensities of love, say, or bitterness, makes it hard to imagine untangling them, allotting them to discrete categories in terms of their physicality or their ideational existence. The bruising that I experience when I am humiliated in front of a loved one is obstinately both literal and metaphorical: I am bruised, I sit slightly slumped, more weary and wary, yet this bruising also reaches inside, I feel internally battered. Could you possibly 'feel' that you were in love if you couldn't also feel your beating heart climbing into your throat or your palms sweat? Would I really be moved by a tragedy if I didn't experience rivulets of tears trickling down my cheeks? The cold, acrid sweat that runs down the side of my body and the bundle of bees nesting in my stomach tell me I am anxious.

Passions have flavours and colours. Bitterness is a taste associated with self-destructive envy and humiliation; sweetness is a flavour of the sentiment attached to cuteness, to a certain sense of love, to innocence (and too much sweetness induces nausea). We call the onset of rage 'the red mist'; the bleakness of melancholia and depression has been likened to a 'black sun' (Kristeva 1989). The writing about the passions, from all the varied perspectives, have always recognised the impossibility of treating the passions as exclusively or even primarily mental or ideational. The passions invite us to treat humans as physical, material beings, dynamically attaching to and extricating from other physical matter. The paradox of the passions is that they seem to be profoundly subjective and expressive, while at the same time they point out to us our thing-like existence (as objects with glands that leak when we are sad, with cheeks that burn when we are embarrassed, with hands that sweat when we are lying, with hearts that quicken when we are excited).

In this section I want to concentrate on David Hume's *A Treatise of Human Nature* (written during 1735 and 1736, then published in three volumes between 1739 and 1740). It is an extraordinary work not least because it was written when Hume was only twenty-five years old (though he claimed to have conceived the project of the book when he was only fourteen, while at university). Hume claimed that the book 'fell dead-born from the Press' (1985 [1739–40]: 17), and while it did receive some favourable endorsements, it was mostly dismissed as innovative but irrelevant and dangerously blasphemous. The subtitle of the *Treatise* gives us a clue as to why it wasn't generally welcomed: *A Treatise of Human Nature: Being an Attempt to Introduce the Experimental Method of Reasoning*. At a time when it was usual to ground philosophical work on the tenets of moral virtue and religious truth, Hume wanted to establish his philosophy on the actuality of experience; to take the methods being established in the natural sciences and apply them to the philosophy of life. So, radically, he starts out from the physical world of sensations, from empirical knowledge of the subject's dynamic relationship with the world around it.

But the *Treatise* is notable not just because it heralds the birth of something new (and there are, as is nearly always the case, important precursors to Hume's work) but also because it marks something of an end for the passions. The *Treatise* marks a transition: it sits between a time more dominated by religious explanation, where the passions might tempt you to stray from the path of righteousness (or, tempered in the right way, help you to this path); and a time (the one we are also living in) when passions give way to more technical explanations of the emotions and the affects as characteristics of social, biological and psychological beings. Certainly for Hume the focus on passion is replaced, in later works, by a concentration on 'moral sentiment'; a move that turns Hume's writing towards a more conventional relationship to eighteenth century philosophy as it was dominantly practised.

While the *Treatise* is full of insights about specific passions, here I just want to look at two ideas which seem to structure Hume's understanding of the passions in general. The first proposal is that the passions are fundamentally different in kind to the world of ideas, and while ideas and passions may constantly interlink, it is worth separating out the world of impressions (which is the more general term Hume gives to sensations and passions) and the world of ideas, as they operate in distinct ways:

> Ideas never admit of a total union, but are endow'd with a kind of impenetrability, by which they exclude each other, and are capable of forming a compound by their conjunction, not by their mixture. On the other hand, impressions and passions are susceptible of an entire union; and like colours, may be blended so perfectly together, that each of them may lose itself, and contribute only to vary that uniform impression, which arises from the whole.
>
> (Hume 1985 [1739–40]: 415)

For Hume there is a reason that we equate the passions with sensations such as taste, colour and sound and this is because of the sort of experience that passionate experience is. Passion is physical but also complexly modulated, with different notes juxtaposed into an overall sound and tone, and with a particular sense of vitality. Hume's point is that it is impossible to think the idea world 'all-at-once', as some sort of subtle blend of thought; instead we work bit-by-bit, adding and synthesising, to create plausible accounts of the world. But the world as an impression can result in a complex blend of sensations and passions; for instance a

7

soldier going into battle might feel fear, anger, uncertainty, excitement, all at once, without any of this feeling contradictory.

Hume isn't suggesting that there is an absolute line that separates ideas and passions; rather, his point is that ideas and passions have characteristic differences that both connect them and differentiate them. And here the part played by energy is crucial:

> Those perceptions, which enter with most force and violence, we may name *impressions*; and under this name I comprehend all our sensations, passions and emotions, as they make their first appearance in the soul. By *ideas* I mean the faint images of these in thinking and reasoning; such as for instance, are all the perceptions excited by the present discourse, excepting only, those which arise from the sight and touch, and excepting the immediate pleasure or uneasiness it may occasion.
>
> (Hume 1985 [1739–40]: 49)

So, even if there are characteristic differences between passion and ideas, there are routes backwards and forwards across them. Thus if ideas have the faint trace of passion and sensation, then it would seem to hold that some ideas will have stronger traces than others. At any rate it would be worth holding on to this point today when certain ideas seem to circulate with such a degree of passionate intensity that the calmness that Hume perceives in the world of ideas seems, in some instances, almost entirely missing.

This two-way path from ideas to passions, and from passions to ideas, is given more substance when we look at the second structural element of Hume's understanding of the passions. For Hume the passions can be divided into two groups: the direct passions and the indirect passions:

> By direct passions I understand such as arise immediately from good or evil, from pleasure or pain. By indirect such as proceed from the same principles, but by the conjunction of other qualities. [...] under the indirect passions I comprehend pride, humility, ambition, vanity, love, hatred, envy, pity, malice, generosity, with their dependents. And under the direct passions, desire, aversion, grief, joy, hope, fear, despair and security.
>
> (Hume 1985 [1739–40]: 328)

Here Hume's point is that the energy that passions carry has an immediate sense of being good or bad, of producing feelings of pleasure or pain. There is no need to read this point in terms

8

of moral judgement (although Hume might have); rather we can see this as the sort of bass-note of experience: does this make you feel good or bad? It is the sort of immediacy of experience that can then be modulated into other passions that Hume calls indirect. Importantly for Hume, as indirect passions are scaffolded onto the initial passion there is, in this scaffolding, a possible route where the passions can become more idea-like, more reflexive (though this doesn't necessarily lessen the energetic charge they carry or excite). For instance, envy might be an indirect passion that initially takes its force from the pleasure that seeing something desirable produces. As an indirect passion envy might build up away from this initially positive energy to fuel negatively charged ideas about the wealth of another.

Hume offers an example of the relationship between direct and indirect passions that give a sense of the complex time factors and energy levels circulating in the world of indirect passions:

> Thus a suit of fine cloaths produces pleasure from their beauty; and this pleasure produces the direct passions, or the impression of volition and desire. Again, when these cloaths are consider'd as belonging to ourself, the double relation conveys to us the sentiment of pride, which is an indirect passion; and the pleasure, which attends that passion, returns back the direct affections, and gives new force to our desire or volition, joy or hope.
>
> (Hume 1985 [1739–40]: 485–6)

So, indirect passions (in this case pride) ride piggy-back on the initial force of pleasure. But pride has its own intensity and this works to increase the force of the direct passion: pleasure is intensified.

This is not the place to fully explore these insights and propositions, but they are worth holding in the back of our minds, if only to constantly remind ourselves that passions are usually messy affairs that carry a range of different, and at times contradictory, elements, and these elements can have wholly different characters (for many, the experience of deep humiliation seems to burn more deeply, and dissipate more slowly than the affective energies of generosity in producing pleasure, for instance). But before we leave the eighteenth century and David Hume behind it is worth looking briefly at the way that thinking about passion was mobilised for particular purposes; as a way of underwriting what Hume would have thought of as a 'calm passion' – the care of money.

Albert Hirschman, in his fascinating book *The Passions and the Interests: Political Arguments for Capitalism before its Triumph*, poses a number of questions that turn out to be central for understanding the emergence of a bold and robust defence of the interests of capitalism. Hirschman's initial problem is how to explain the movement from a time when avarice was considered one of the most vulgar passions (and when glory-seeking, for instance, was given a much stronger endorsement as a vice or passion that could produce good and noble deeds) to a time when a certain amount of avarice was seen as a practical necessity. The movement that Hirschman maps is one set in the seventeenth and eighteenth century, a time when 'moralizing philosophy and religious precept could no longer be trusted with restraining the destructive passions of men' (Hirschman 1997 [1977]: 14–15). The complex narrative that Hirschman tells is one that works across a number of writers (including Hume) and which takes us into our present time.

The problem for seventeenth and eighteenth century European thought highlights the centrality of the passions at this time. Given the strength of the passions, and given the lack of authority being exercised by the moralising of religion and philosophy, what do you do to check the passions? Or in another vein; given how unreasonable the passions are, how do you make them more reasonable? It is, of course, a problem that is paradoxical, and the answer it received was equally paradoxical: you set passions against passions, fight fire with fire. The argument that Hume and others made was that the only thing strong enough to fight passion is passion. Relatively benign passions must be used to block the corrosive effects of other passions: self-love could be seen as a reasonable passion to be set against the seemingly baser passion of lust. This is Claude Adrien Helvétius writing in 1758 giving an example of how one passion might be used to block another:

> Only a passion can triumph over a passion; that, for example, if one wishes to induce more modesty and restraint in a forward woman (*femme galante*) one ought to set her vanity against her coquetry and make realize that modesty is an invention of love and refined voluptuousness...
> (Helvétius cited in Hirschman 1997 [1977]: 28)

So at the same time that the passions take centre stage in discussions of human nature, they are being instrumentalised for the pursuit of moral, ideological and economical ends (in this case the ideological task of restraining female sexuality).

Hirschman's story is centrally about the recoding of certain low-intensity passions as interests. Interests are passions rebranded, so to speak, as necessary evils, as forms of human fallibility that can be directed towards good ends. By the eighteenth century and on into the twentieth century any number of thinkers can be found taking passions such as avarice, ambition, and vanity and refashioning them as interests necessary to maintain the 'common good'. Of course it is not hard to see from our place in history that this recoding was motivated in the interests of particular groups (and given the importance of interests, this is hardly a contradiction) and that lustful women, sensualists, bohemians and those who didn't produce wealth, are going to be particularly demonised by this discourse. It is quite a feat, however to turn avarice into a moral good, to see commerce as a major force for good (the example that is often used is that two countries doing good business with each other are hardly likely to go to war). Of course the story of the last three hundred years is not one of calm passions blocking the murderous desires of the violent passions. Avarice was unleashed, and the story of civilisation must be seen, at some level, as a story of unconstrained greed. Rather than tempering other passions, the re-branding of profiteering works to allow murderous hatreds, fear and anger to piggy-back on what gets written as a fundamental of human nature: the desire for gain.

ETHOS

During the centuries that followed the eighteenth century, passions don't go away but are continually recoded and reanimated. For my purposes one of the more interesting and useful ways that the passions get recoded is shown in the work of Gregory Bateson. Working as an anthropologist in the 1930s (he would later turn his hand to a number of other endeavours like cybernetics and the study of schizophrenia) Gregory Bateson proposed an opposition for understanding the workings of culture that usefully connects to the privileging of passion that I've been keen to foster here. Culture, for Bateson, was composed of both 'eidos' and 'ethos'. In a rough and ready way eidos designates the logic of culture, forms of cognition, and social structure (varied institutional arrangements, such as marriage, the family, the state). Ethos, on the other hand, was emotion, manner and tone. It is probably too much of an absolute division to work for long and Bateson knew that in actuality these two aspects were 'fundamentally inseparable'; nevertheless it allowed Bateson the space to pursue aspects crucial to the study of passionate culture. Echoing David Hume he writes: 'Since, however, it is impossible to present the whole of a culture simultaneously in a single flash, I must begin at some arbitrarily chosen point' (Bateson 1958 [1936]: 3). For Bateson, as for us, this meant starting with ethos, with passionate culture.

While ethos exists in ordinary language (we talk about a 'group ethos', or a particular corporation as having their own, particular ethos, like, 'play hard and work harder'), Bateson means something at once more intricate and more expansive by the term. Ethos is Bateson's central concern, to the point where he will describe his methodology as ethological. The 'ethological' approach is premised on the idea: 'that we may abstract from a culture a certain systematic aspect called ethos which we may define as the expression of *a culturally standardised system of organisation of the instincts and emotions of the individuals'* (Bateson 1958 [1936]: 118 italics in the original). Today we might be more wary of exactly how standardised a system of instincts and emotions could be within groups that are often structured around gender differences or class distinctions or generational change. Nonetheless Bateson's point is that many of the defining aspects of cultural life are to be found at the level of ethos.

The example that he uses to explain the materiality of ethos is tellingly specific:

> When a group of young intellectual English men or women are talking and joking together wittily and with a touch of light cynicism, there is established among them for the time being a definite tone of appropriate behaviour. Such specific tones of behaviour are in all cases indicative of an ethos. They are expressions of a standardised system of emotional attitudes. In this case the men have temporarily adopted a definite set of sentiments

towards the rest of the world, a definite attitude towards reality, and they will joke about subjects which at another time they would treat with seriousness.

(Bateson 1958 [1936]: 19)

We might note in passing how Bateson is careful not to include men *and* women in his example. Yet the crucial move that Bateson makes is to treat passion (the sentiments that circulate in an ethos) as primarily cultural. It is not simply me responding to the world with pleasure and pain, but of me being placed within a culture where passions circulate, and where I am impassioned in a whole host of ways.

David Hume's work is (consciously or not) echoed in the way Bateson describes ethos. His words sound like musical tunings ('definite tone of appropriate behaviour') or discussions of painterly effects ('an emotional background'). Emotional tonality is the privileged way of describing ethos for Bateson. While Hume tends to describe passions as they affect one person (a single person connecting to the world), ethos is always communal passion (an ethos that applied to one person would be a contradiction in terms). The sense of an ethos that might belong to a very large group (a nation, a generation) is always going to be an abstraction, yet within its abstract surface lies real concrete elements; ways of greeting (hugs, handshakes, kisses, etc.); forms of perceiving (social recognition and misrecognition of class, caste, gender, sexuality and so on); affective intensity (the permission, or not, to be angry, the uses of humiliation, etc.); and so on. Ethos may well best be approached as something like a tonality, or a feeling, but its polyphonic dimension, its complexity, must be continually stressed.

Bateson's ethos is the performance of a communal passionate culture on a day to day basis. We only tend to notice it when it goes wrong, when we feel uncomfortable or when the ethos is unknown to us. It takes a particularly confident or arrogant person to enter an unknown ethos and to feel immediately comfortable. As Bateson's suggests, a degree of tuning is required to get the ethos right. In various places in society there are rituals of induction (in religious systems, in educational institutions) as well as what might be described as tacit tuning (the first years of school establish all sorts of 'tones of appropriate behaviour' both in the classroom and in the playground). But while ethos is a fascinating aspect of culture to follow in its own right, for Bateson there was a more compelling task for an ethological orientation to pursue. What happens when two passionate cultures collide, or coincide? What might occur during an ethological clash? If ethos, unlike eidos, has no recourse to forms of rational persuasion ('we do things in this way as it rains for eleven months a year') then how is ethos negotiated in cultural encounters?

In late 1935, with one eye probably on the rise of fascism in Europe and the other on the role that anthropology has played as an arm of colonial administration, Gregory Bateson outlined a research project for the study of schismogenesis. Schismogenesis is Bateson's name for forms of acculturation (the cultural processes arising form the meeting of distinct cultural groups or cultural factions) which, often aggressively, result in the intensification of cultural differences or cultural rivalry. While Bateson is clear that cultural interchange can result in 'acceptance and adaptation' and in forms of 'approximate equilibrium', he is – in 1935 – particularly interested in, and aware of, 'drastic disturbances which follow contacts between profoundly different communities' (Bateson 1935: 179). For Bateson the study of schismogenesis would be an essential project for a class of expert social scientists whose job it would be to inform political administrators.

Schismogenesis is Bateson puzzling to understand how and why groups don't undergo some sort of cultural osmosis when they come into contact with one another, why cultural mixing doesn't result in 'melting pot' cultures, and why distinction and rivalry are often intensified through contact. Of course, he is not naïve enough to forget that cultural contact is nearly always forged under conditions of violent domination, but he is also enough of an anthropologist to have examples of cultures where antagonistic intergroup contact is an essential element of their general lifeworld. Schismogenesis is Bateson's initial attempt to bring a form of systems theory to bear on social life. For Bateson there are two (often overlapping) forms of schismogenesis: symmetrical schismogenesis and complementary schismogenesis. Acculturation often leads 'toward more intense rivalry in the case of symmetrical schismogenesis, or toward increasing differentiation of role in complementary schismogenesis' (Bateson 1958 [1936]: 285). After the

Second World War the spectacular proliferation of nuclear weapons by the protagonists in the cold war offered a vivid example of symmetrical schismogenesis. Generally symmetrical schismogenesis occurred and occurs between two separate units that encounter one another (nation states, tribal groups, etc.). Complementary schismogenesis is more ubiquitous, Bateson sees it occurring between genders within communities, between the old and the young, and we could see it as a form of class distinction, where class differences intensify at moments of close proximity. In contemporary multicultural society complementary schismogenesis is perhaps even more visible.

Distinctions between symmetrical and complementary schismogenesis are hard to maintain for long: it is hard, for instance, to see something like the cold war as not intensifying difference (ideological and cultural) at the same time as rivalry. Similarly the idea that forms of complementary schismogenesis don't also entail forms of rivalry is also difficult to sustain. What is more important, though, is the way Bateson understands the conditions necessary for schismogenesis to occur: after all it is perfectly possible for schismogenesis not to occur. For Bateson schismogenesis is dependent on the particular 'ethos' of a group. Ethos, to borrow a term from Jacques Rancière, could be thought of as the 'distribution of the sensible' (*le partage du sensible*): 'the system of *a priori* forms determining what presents itself to sense experience. It is a delimitation of spaces and times, of the visible and the invisible, of speech and noise, that simultaneously determines the place and stakes of politics as a form of experience' (Rancière 2004: 13). Ethos, then, would be the orchestration of perception, of the sentiments and emotional orientations, and so on: more pertinently it will be the interlacing of these. Forms and techniques of personal hygiene, for instance, or food preparation, might differ between two cultures. Such differences might be the site of friction when two cultures meet or need to coexist. From this might come a rudimentary understanding of schismogenesis. Ethos allows you to see why and how a particular style of washing matters; it links the perception of cleanliness and dirt, or purity and impurity, to orchestrations of shame and comfort, to resonances of other sensual worlds, and on to the social understanding of human bodies.

Bateson's work connects us back to an earlier understanding of cultural life that saw the passions, not as the froth surfacing from something more solid and profound, but as the central component of creaturely comfort. Such an orientation allows us to see how something as seemingly innocuous as taste might matter. Why differences in tastes might provoke aggressive and violent clashes, or sympathetic appreciation. But if ethos is, for Bateson, an object of knowledge, it might also be useful to think of it as a component of knowledge, a necessary condition of how we know the world.

PASSIONATE KNOWING

In academia, the scholarly life is often premised on the suppression of passion. Historians are warned about over-identification with their subject matter; students of literature are taught to radically temper their emotional responses, in case they make an 'affective fallacy' (getting all weepy is considered decidedly unprofessional). Those in the social sciences are given countless safeguards to stop the passions encroaching on the business of producing reliable knowledge, while the harder sciences make a value out of everything the passions are not: testable, logical, rational. Even those areas of inquiry more dedicated to the passions (psychology, say) find ways of investigating the passions dispassionately. Of course there is nothing wrong, in a sense, with these values. Anyone who has had a conversation with someone who is immersed in all-consuming sentimentality knows how circuitous such discussion can be, and anyone trying to reason with a child having a tantrum will know the futility of such an endeavour (much better to retune their passion through distraction). My argument is not that the values of dispassion are bad, simply that they are disingenuous and obscuring of many of the ways we know the world, including scholarly knowledge.

One of the reasons for Descartes placing 'wonder' as the primary passion is, I think, due to its capacity to produce knowledge. Wonder, as Philip Fisher describes it (with reference to Spinoza), is a passionate state of not knowing: 'wonder as a kind of stalling of the mind in front of something in which the novelty is so striking that it does not lead to any associations that would bring the mind to connect it and move back and forth from one object to the other' (Fisher 2002: 29). Not knowing is the necessary pre-

condition of new knowledge, of finding out something new. Without it, as Fisher suggests, we move 'back and forth from one object
to the other' caught in the world of the already known, the world
of received wisdom, the same ol', same ol'. Knowledge, of course,
is still possible here, but it is the knowledge of minor adjustments
and nuanced interpretation. The drive for knowledge, for Fisher
(and for Spinoza and Descartes in their different ways) is found in
that stalling of the mind, of the mind's enchantment in the face of
something that it is unable to immediately process.

Wonder and curiosity have been a fundamental condition for knowledge. In their excellent *Wonders and the Order of Nature* Lorraine
Daston and Katharine Park explore the condition of wonder (and
what made something wonderful) during the period 1150–1750.
They show how wonder has a history, how it was at times aligned
with passions like curiosity and horror and at other points distinct.
Wonder differed depending on who was wondering, who was full of
wonder:

> In the hand of medieval abbots and princes, natural wonders such
> as ostrich eggs, magnets, and carbuncles represented the wealth
> of their possessors and their power over the natural and the
> human world. In the hands of philosophers, theologians, and phys-
> icians, they were recondite objects of specialised knowledge
> that transcended prosaic experience. In the hands of sixteenth-
> and seventeenth-century virtuosi and collectors, they became occa-
> sions for elaborate exercises in taste and connoisseurship.
> (Daston and Park 2001: 19)

Contemporary academic scholarship might be seen to manage wonder too, but also to cool it and temper it. In a more positive light
it might also be seen as democratising it, loosening the role of
wealthy elites and replacing them with technical specialists whose
task is to disseminate knowledge.

While wonder and curiosity might seem to be passion's natural
brokers of knowledge (or the path to knowledge) what might other
passions teach us? What could we know through trepidation, fear
and anger? Trepidation, and trepidation's colleague tentativeness,
could be seen as the necessary requirements of scepticism. And
without scepticism, without the nagging apprehensiveness of doubt,
modern science would have had a hard time loosening its ties with
dogmatic religious belief. While science has its fair share of acts of

what could we know through disgust/shame? – boundaries/self **17** faith (mathematics, for instance, can claim something as being simultaneously true and unverifiable) it has also installed sceptical hesitancy as a positive value.

The shape of knowledge in the human sciences has, since the 1960s, been fundamentally transformed by a number of disciplinary interventions. Mobilising a long heritage and a rich range of radical thought (that had been hovering on the borders of academic life), interventions such as feminism, post-colonialism, queer theory, critical race studies, history-from-below, and other fields of interventionist inquiry, have all challenged received wisdoms. Fields of knowledge which had happily paraded terms like 'genius' were revealed to be operating a patriarchal logic (see Battersby 1989, for example); historians who had assumed that the true agents of history were politicians and elites were confronted with another side of the story (Linebaugh and Rediker 2000, as well as countless other books). Many of these interventions were driven by anger at the way so few people, and so few kinds of experience, were given any expressive space in the academy or in social life more generally. But if anger was a rightful element within these inquiries it rarely exhausted or even characterised the passionate knowledge being produced.

Feminism might be seen as exemplary here (though it is clearly difficult to characterise this as a single field) and can be seen to passionately animate knowledge in a number of ways. If an underlying energy motivating feminism could be seen as anger, or purposive pride in the face of too many centuries of humiliation, then this energy props up and is recoded by any number of other passionate forms: generosity (an opening out towards others); hope (the reanimating of anger and fear as a positive cast towards the future) and so on. Yet, no doubt, there would also be other, less positive passions in circulation that might have little to do specifically with feminism and everything to do with the ethos of a particular professional culture (though of course feminism would clearly be available as an analytic approach to such an ethos).

There is not room here to itemise all the passionate ways of knowing that have driven scholarly inquiry, or the space to map out the varied productivities of passionate knowing. My point is, simply, that all knowing is energised (for both ill and good) by passion, and that it is better to start out with such an acknowledgement than to try and suppress it through blind allegiance to scientific protocols and academic manners. This is not to suggest that wilful ways of knowing the world can pass as scholarship, merely to say that there is no scholarship without passion.

In what follows while there are no ostrich eggs or magnets, there are things to marvel at (in awe, in disbelief, in recognition). For the most part the passions that we see here are not the vehement passions in all their intensity, but the ethological passions of emotional tones, of passionate discord, of the passions utilised by finance capital. Passionate culture is always to some degree a shared arena (this is the definition of the term culture) – though who shares it and how far this sharing goes is always a central question for cultural studies. Some of the passions we look at seem more like moods: the forms of unease and melancholy that can be generated by modern technologies of communication, for instance.

I've chosen passionate culture as a way of getting into, and getting on with, the study of culture. I have already mentioned how the markets have been responding to the passions of unease and fear and how this spread like an emotional contagion across so many countries as I was writing this book. Yet out of that generalised sense of anxiety new passions are emerging and will emerge. For the first time in decades the mainstream media is signalling a doubt about the certainty of unregulated capitalism as the only way of running the world; people are seeing the collapse of so many avarice-motivated institutions as an opportunity to do things differently to try and aim towards global solutions to world inequality and climate change. If the long history of the modern has reanimated the passions for the purposes of self-interest, perhaps it is time to reignite the passions for an outward looking, more benevolent aim. At any rate to leave out passionate culture when delineating a politics of hope would be, I am convinced, a mistake.

2 Bitter Tastes

(On discernment, disgust, and shame)

In this chapter I suggest that taste is a central organiser of passionate culture. While traditionally taste has been seen as one of the ways people experience class and other social differences, I want to show that there is a sense in which taste defines the very edges of what culture is (and isn't). This is particularly evident when we stop thinking about good and bad taste and instead think about literal aspects of taste, like disgust and revulsion, and their opposite, carnal relish. In this chapter we meet the biologist Charles Darwin, the critical journalist George Orwell and the novelists Timothy Mo and Jonathan Frazen.

Enter any large music store and you are confronted with a selection of genres: easy listening; rap and hip hop; reggae; heavy metal; R&B and soul; classical; jazz and so on. Heading for one area rather than another is a way of signalling your preferences, your taste, your discrimination and discernment. We all have preferences, likes and dislikes but why would any of these preferences matter in the larger scheme of things (I like peas, you like cheese; what of it)? Ask a small child what their favourite colour is, or what their best meal would be, and they often have a ready answer. How could you argue against the colour red or against spaghetti?

During 1993 and 1994, the Russian-American artists Vitaly Komar and Alexander Melamid, using professional polling firms, consulted nearly two billion people (nearly a third of the world's population) about their taste preferences in the area of fine art. From these finding Komar and Melamid produced two paintings for each national poll: the country's most wanted painting and their most unwanted one (Wypijewski 1999). The paintings were syntheses of the polls, standardising general likings for recognisable pictures of nature over hard-edged abstractions, for instance, or for soft blues, greens and browns, over spiky oranges, pinks, and purples. Yet what the project demonstrated was the impossibility of accessing passionate taste at such a level of generality: the most wanted paintings, in trying to satisfy everyone, satisfied nobody (and this was Komar and Melamid's joke, as much as it was poking fun at the seriousness of the art business).

Yet taste is not simply an arena for the pleasures involved in having preferences; it can also be one of anxiety, humiliation and exclusion. Personally I don't like cotton-wool. Actually that's not quite right: I have an aversion to cotton-wool. Show me some cotton-wool, or worse, squeeze it in front of me or make me touch it, and I start to shiver, to ice-over inside. I have a dis-taste for cotton-wool but is this taste of the same register as having a liking for modernist furniture or the architecture of Antoni Gaudi, or for thinking that the art of Andy Warhol will never measure up to that of Michelangelo? I love the music of Robert Wyatt, I love his quirky voice, his eclectic range of musical motifs; but I'm happy enough for you to tell me that you don't love it, that you find his voice insipid, his music too meandering and his politics just too evident. None of this necessarily matters culturally: these are personal passions. For taste to become part of passionate culture more generally it has got to connect with larger passions.

What if my love of something had the effect of humiliating you, of belittling your musical tastes? What if you decided that anyone who belonged to your group had to share your taste, or that anyone who liked Wyatt's music couldn't join your group or be friends with anyone in the group? What if my cotton-wool distaste was shared; a common reaction of revulsion towards the cotton-wool-loving group who lived across the river? This revulsion towards cotton-wool would not only make it cultural – it would also show how formations of taste (and more importantly of distaste) get under the skin, appear as a fact of the body rather than of opinion. Of course taste is rarely as explicit as this; most of the time it sits around in a fairly take-it-or-leave-it manner ('beauty is in the eye of the beholder', 'there's no accounting for taste', 'you can't dispute taste' and so on). But partly because it doesn't claim to be logical, or even reasonable, taste accomplishes powerful cultural provocation and persuasion. It provokes and persuades because, in a certain way, taste is simply unanswerable.

Thinkers in eighteenth century England and Scotland seem to have been obsessed with questions of taste. For writers like the third Earl of Shaftesbury (Anthony Ashley Cooper) taste, mediated by philosophy, was a way of managing unruly passions: 'Tis the known Province of Philosophy to teach us *our-selves*, keep us the *self-same* Persons, and so regulate our governing Fancys, Passions, and Humours' (Shaftesbury 1710 cited in Porter 2004: 137). Shaftesbury imagined a civilising process dedicated to taste that would require both innate sensitivity to the products of divine beauty (to be found, in the main, in nature) as well as the cultivation of behaviour and appreciation, that would produce 'a polite Man of Taste' (Gigante 2005: 49). Taste required moral as well as sensual discrimination and nowhere was this more evident than in the production of tasteful manners: forms of politeness and decorum, the eradication of any gross or rude conduct, the establishing of forms of etiquette, and so on. Taste at this time was much more forcefully linked to its gustatory roots, to taste as sensuous enjoyment as well as to a refusal to succumb to the appetites (lust, gluttony, and so on).

Eighteenth century philosophers wrestled with the possibility of discerning laws of taste – rules for recognising beauty (even if the rule of law might turn out to suggest that beauty was self-evident) as well as for complying with social protocols. But these rules couldn't simply be obeyed: they had to be embodied and, to some degree, inherited. As Roy Porter suggests, for Shaftesbury:

> Loveliness [...] was objectively real, it was the splendour of the divine nature about which he rhapsodized; but appreciation of such loveliness was not something any Tom, Dick or Harry instinctively experienced or had the right to pronounce upon; while seeded in the human heart, it needed cultivation. Taste involved not only an exquisite, intuitive discrimination beyond mechanical calculation, but also a relish verging on enthusiasm: aesthetic transports implied a participation in the grander cosmic whole, transcending gross self-gratification.
>
> (Porter 2001: 163–4)

In one sense this had the effect of disseminating 'gentlemanly' conduct (and the gendering of this conduct was far from arbitrary) and of promoting the taste culture of those who could claim 'intuitive discrimination' (the elite tastemakers of the day).

Writing about eighteenth century taste and the way it can be seen as embodying the values and aspirations of the dominant classes, Terry Eagleton comments:

> 'Civilized' conduct takes its cue from traditional aristocratism: its index is the fluent, spontaneous, taken-for-granted virtue of the gentleman, rather than the earnest conformity to some external law of the petty bourgeois. Moral standards, while still implacably absolute in themselves, may thus be to some extent diffused into the textures of personal sensibility: taste, affect and opinion testify more eloquently to one's participation in a universal common sense then either moral strenuousness or ideological doctrine.
>
> (Eagleton 1990: 32)

Eagleton's point is that taste is a form of social governing that works by looking as if it places all responsibility in the hands (and bodies) of the individual's subjectivity, yet it does this so long as these subjectivities conform to an idea of 'common sense' (common sensibility and sentiment).

Yet this suggestion of taste laws seems to imply that eighteenth century Britain was a stable society. In fact it is much closer to us than we might at first assume. One way of understanding all this talk of taste and decorum is as a reaction to change: to change in social classes (the emergence of middle classes); the expansion of consumer society and the forces of fashion; and the challenge to traditions and social conventions. You get a sense of the reactive work of taste in the subtitle of the painter William Hogarth's 1753 book *The Analysis of Beauty: Written with a view of fixing the fluctuating Ideas of Taste* (cited in Hooker 1934: 578). And it is fashion as much as anything (fashions of conduct, dress, eating, and so on) that would puncture any claim to the stability of taste, or any claim for some continuous level of aesthetic value. Or as Walter Benjamin writes: 'Each generation experiences the fashions of the one immediately preceding it as the most radical antiaphrodisiac imaginable' (Benjamin 1999: 79).

But if nothing undoes the belief in the laws of taste more than fashion, nothing relies more on this belief than fashion. The fashion houses want our passionate commitment to their latest offerings, to recognise their innate tastefulness, but as soon as we commit ourselves we are in danger of being caught out as unfashionable, of wearing last year's style. In 1954 the managing editor of

Harper's Magazine (a US general interest magazine) suggested that instead of looking to see what is and isn't tasteful it would be more useful to look to see who it is that is wielding the power of taste (Lynes 1954). Certainly today it is worth looking to see the extent of what we might call the taste industry and to see how this industry calls on our passions to function. Lifestyle magazines and TV, for instance, motivate us through envy, fear, greed, desire, and surprise to be interested in what they have to say and what they have to offer: TV programmes telling you what to wear and what not to wear and how to look good naked; magazines telling me what my house should look like; adverts scaring me about my health or rather my lack of it; more TV telling you what to eat, how to treat your children, how to get on and how to get by, how to have the x-factor, how to be satisfied, how to achieve more, how to relax more. Seen as a collective enterprise the taste industry might make you feel what Henri Lefebvre called the twofold terrorism of daily life: be like this, or you'll be like that (Lefebvre 1984 [1968]: 106).

The myriad tentacles of the taste industry suggest that the ideal addressee of this industry is not Shaftesbury's Man of Taste, but the profligate, forgetful and promiscuous consumer – someone whose passionate commitments are short-lived, someone whose dietary loyalties are easily challenged. Recent sociological research in North America shows that the most affluent and 'high-status' citizens do not exhibit singular taste and discernment; they express instead an omnivorous appetite for all sorts of cultural material (Peterson and Kern 1996). If the Man of Taste was a snob who feared being polluted by low behaviour, low taste, the new taste economy positively encourages a promiscuous sampling across taste domains.

The term 'taste', often centre-stage in evaluative aesthetic discourse, vividly registers the co-mingling of sense and status, of discernment and disdain, of the physical and the mental. The very use of the word 'taste' to describe refined and discerning choice (and the social status that might go with it) should alert us to the way that bodily sensual life is implied in such judgements from the start. Given the privileging of the 'higher' senses (hearing and seeing, but also touch) in the history of Western thought it might seem that the very idea of 'taste' to signify discernment is already flirting with distaste by invoking the 'lower' senses (smell and taste). One aspect of this distribution of sense (both mental and sensual) is the way that seeing and hearing are invoked in matters of mental cognition ('ah, I see', 'I hear you'), whereas 'taste' uses the sensual realms which are, in the end, impervious to rationalist dictates.

Taste is an orchestration of the sensual and passionate world, a way of ordering and demeaning, of giving value and taking it away. On one level it seems to occupy a thin level of culture (the preoccupation of critics, gourmands, and the like); on another it will seem as the very basis of culture, not simply its system of values but the way that set of values gets under your skin and into your bones. While it might seem an overstatement to suggest that groups might go to war over taste disputes, it is hard to imagine that what we term culture is not in the end (and endlessly) driven by the peculiar admix of status, sensual perception, and passionate culture that is instanced by taste.

In this chapter, though, I want to look at taste, less as a wilful choice (say, Shakespeare versus Kylie, or Rembrandt versus Anime), and more as an anxious and seemingly ingrained state. This is not to say that Shakespeare or Kylie Minogue might not be part of your ingrained, intimate world of taste, just that, for passionate culture, taste is more often intensely felt as the feeling that distaste provokes (how hurt would feel if someone fell asleep in *Hamlet* or talked while Kylie's *Wow* was playing?). As Pierre Bourdieu suggests:

> In matters of taste, more than anywhere else, all determination is negation; and tastes are perhaps first and foremost distastes, disgust provoked by horror or visceral intolerance ('sick-making') of the tastes of others. [...] Aesthetic intolerance can be terribly violent. Aversion to different lifestyles is perhaps one of the strongest barriers between the classes.
>
> (Bourdieu 1992 [1979]: 56)

Cultural taste is intimate and feels ingrained (feels like it constitutes the grain of the fabric of your being) at the point where its challenge threatens the necessary characteristics of your selfhood.

THE ANXIETY OF TASTE

Taste is a perilous business. It is hedged in from all sides by the physical possibility of revulsion, disgust and disdain. Who can be certain of their taste? As David Hume made clear in the mid-eighteenth century: 'We are apt to call *barbarous* whatever departs widely from our own taste and apprehension; but soon find the epithet of reproach retorted on us' (Hume 1757: 134). But if we are socially vulnerable in our discernment, that vulnerability is intensified by a passionate pull that makes taste matter in very specific ways. After all distaste is not simply disagreement: even in its mildest form it involves the wrinkling of noses, turning the head away and so on. At its most extreme distaste is actual revolt (the body's revolt); physical nausea, vomiting, and retching. In ordinary circumstances distaste is signalled through a register of passions sliding from condescension, to disdain, through to scorn and contempt: how could you possibly have imagined that this disgusting item would be appealing to me? Disdain, then (as the most general mode of showing distaste) is one way of inflicting cultural pain, and it is most effective when emotional interest is involved and where reassurance is sought. Disdain works to push away and to ruin simultaneously.

Jonathan Franzen's ambitious novel *The Corrections* provides, among other things, an emotional vivisection of a white, North American, Midwestern, middle class, elderly couple, and the more sophisticated and metropolitan lives of their children. A sprawling novel that chillingly portrays disintegrating mental states as well as international financial networks, *The Corrections* is constantly weaving links between mentalities and markets. While none of the characters are conventionally sympathetic, one of the least sympathetically drawn characters is the mother Enid. Taste matters for Enid; and it matters so considerably because she is never quite certain of her taste, or rather, of the status of her taste in the wider world. Within the confines of her home she can wield taste as a weapon in the constant war of her disappointing marriage. Her husband, who has retired and is suffering from Parkinson's disease, has bought his first piece of furniture, a vast blue leather armchair. The chair provokes Enid to the point where she redecorates their sitting room so as to have an excuse for expelling the chair:

> Enid looked at the chair. Her expression was merely pained, no more. "I never liked that chair."
> This was probably the most terrible thing she could have said to Alfred. The chair was the only sign he'd ever given of having a personal vision of the future. Enid's words filled him with such sorrow – he felt such pity for the chair, such solidarity with it, such

astonished grief at its betrayal – that he pulled off the dropcloth and sank into its arms and fell asleep.

(Franzen 2001: 11)

(Franzen's book is, as you might have gathered, something of a black comedy.) Here, taste is more than status or a display of cultural capital, it is cultural power played out on a violently and bodily plane.

This chair brings to mind other chairs. In the US TV comedy *Frasier*, a sophisticated Seattle radio psychiatrist (Frasier) lives with his blue-collar, ex-police officer dad (Martin) and his live-in physiotherapist (Daphne) in a swanky tastefully designed apartment. Martin has one piece of furniture, an ill-repaired, sickly green barcalounger, patched-up with carpet tape. The chair sits there in this immaculate apartment, constantly puncturing Frasier's taste-dream and sticking out like the proverbial sore thumb. And as if this isn't enough the chair is positioned in a way that declares its use: it is pointed towards the TV. Throughout the early series of this long running sitcom Frasier was constantly finding ways of disposing of the chair, of trying to eradicate what to him was an eyesore and a constant infraction of his taste regime. Yet the chair kept returning. While Martin was sometimes galled by his son's disdain for the chair he was never hurt the way Alfred was: my guess is that Martin always recognised the anxiety and insecurity that such obsessive interior design suggests (see Highmore 2001).

Enid (to return to *The Corrections*) knows how to use taste to wound because she is constantly aware of how it would be possible for certain people (most specifically her daughter, Denise) to completely undo her through taste and distaste:

> Enid had, true enough, had fun at Dean and Trish's party, and she'd wished that Denise had been there to see for herself how elegant it was. At the same time, she was afraid that Denise would not have found the party elegant at all, that Denise would have picked apart its specialness until there was nothing left but ordinariness. Her daughter's taste was a dark spot in Enid's vision, a hole in her experience through which her own pleasures were forever threatening to leak and dissipate.
>
> (Franzen 2001: 113)

Denise can wield such power in matters of taste, not simply because she has left the Midwest for the seemingly more sophisticated pastures of the Eastern Seaboard, but because she has become head-chef at Philadelphia's coolest restaurant. Haute-cuisine, even in the pseudo-rustic casual elegance of its contemporary performance, is tastefulness in a pristine but dogmatic state. The strong relationship between food and taste is not simply based on the metaphoric association of 'taste' with discernment. Rather food is the *sine qua non* of taste's emotional function. Not only does food provide so many opportunities for the production of shame and humiliation in the face of social ignorance and squeamishness (not being sufficiently knowledgeable about food) as well as biological uncouthness (not having a sensitive palate), it intensifies such production because food is orchestrated around the body (its surfaces, its interiors, its ingestions).

The recipient of disdain, or worse, disgust feels shame. This is Bourdieu's point about the violence of 'aesthetic intolerance'. Of course shame doesn't just require the look of contempt, disgust or disdain to set it in motion; we have enough internalised anxiety to imagine the disdain of our bungled attempts to fit in, be part of things, share tastes. In Sylvia Plath's 1963 novel *The Bell Jar* the protagonist attends a posh grown-up dinner party. After an entrée the waiters bring around small bowls of water with petals floating in them. The protagonist mistakes a finger bowl (for rinsing her fingers) for a very thin soup and proceeds to consume it; when she realises her mistake she seems to crumple from within; cast low by the feeling of deep shame.

Taste and the negative responses it implies (here disdain) is, as we have seen, a product of class or aspirational differences (Alfred had managed to provide a vision of the future that didn't coincide with Enid's aspirations). In Plath's novel the parochial protagonist strays into the taste culture of another class, a more metropolitan, more sophisticated group. But while these taste clashes may sting deeply or provoke anxiety they do not register the full effects of what Bateson meant by schismogenesis (discussed in the previous chapter). For this we have to look at clashes that highlight the rupturing effects of seemingly incompatible taste regimes.

CROSS-CULTURAL FLAVOURS

One of the most vivid, visceral descriptions of disgust belongs to the psychoanalyst Julia Kristeva. This is Kristeva writing in what appears to be an autobiographical vein about 'her' disgust for the creamy layer that was often found on the top of full-fat milk:

> Food loathing is perhaps the most elementary and most archaic form of abjection. When the eyes see or the lips touch that skin on the surface of milk – harmless, then as a sheet of cigarette paper, pitiful as a nail paring – I experience a gagging sensation and, still further down, spasms in the stomach, the belly; and all the organs shrivel up the body, provoke tears and bile, increase heartbeat, cause forehead and hands to perspire. Along with sight-clouding dizziness, *nausea* makes me balk at that milk cream, separates me from the mother and father who proffer it.
>
> (Kristeva 1982: 2–3)

For Kristeva, here, disgust at the abject is an automatic reflex, not a decision that comes from conscious thought. Yet it is precisely because disgust is aimed at alien matter (matter that threatens her, that seems to threaten her body and the borders of her subjectivity), that shows it is neither purely biological nor wilfully individual (a mere matter of idiosyncrasy). An abject response to milk, like my responses to cotton-wool, makes it into a foreign, utterly 'other' thing.

In an interview Kristeva glosses the French term for the abject in the following way:

> *L'abjection* is something that disgusts you, for example, you see something rotting and you want to vomit – it is an extremely strong feeling that is at once somatic and symbolic, which is above all a revolt against an external menace from which one wants to distance oneself, but of which one has the impression that it may menace us from the inside.
>
> (Kristeva 1996: 118)

This sense that what disgusts is both a part of oneself and something that you just want to push away from you is, I think, crucial to the strong passionate feelings that elements of disgust arouse. And it is when this is played-out across and between cultures that it appears most intense and most precarious.

In 1872 Charles Darwin, the theorist of evolution and the writer of *The Origin of the Species* (1859), published his much less renowned book *The Expression of the Emotions in Man and*

Animals. He doesn't write that much about disgust but his initial example is suggestively rich. This is Darwin:

> The term 'disgust', in its simplest sense, means something offensive to the taste. It is curious how readily this feeling is excited by anything unusual in the appearance, odour, or nature of our food. In Tierra del Fuego a native touched with his finger some cold preserved meat which I was eating at our bivouac and plainly showed utter disgust at its softness; whilst I felt utter disgust at my food being touched by a naked savage, though his hands did not appear dirty. A smear of soup on a man's beard looks disgusting, though there is nothing disgusting in the soup itself.
> (Darwin 1999 [1872]: 255)

Here, then, what disgusts are practices and matter felt to be alien, felt to be out of place, and connecting us all too closely to other bodies, other people (the soup on the beard too emphatically points to the lips, to the material processes of another person eating, another person digesting).

William Ian Miller's book, *The Anatomy of Disgust*, begins by examining Darwin's short discussion of disgust and shows that while disgust works both ways (both the adventurer Darwin and the native of Tierra del Fuego are disgusted), it works unevenly. If disgust takes its power from the ability of the object to disrupt, corrupt and contaminate then Darwin and the native are choosing different objects: what is contaminating for Darwin is the (clean) touch by a naked black man; for the native of Tierra del Fuego it is the disruption of food categories, embodied in the soft cold meat that disgusts (rather than the body and person of Darwin).

Even this micro-scene should (again) alert us to the fact that disgust is cultural rather than natural (though certain smells provoke an almost universal sense of disgust). Miller argues that while our reaction to tastes and smells seem automatic and disinterested, we have only to think of moments when our reflex reaction has altered in response to changes in comprehension (when, for instance, you are told that what you are enjoying eating is not what you thought it was) to have a sense of how mutable and motivated our sense perceptions are:

> Yet our senses, even our olfactory sense, are manipulable and markedly affected by our beliefs. Many bad odors become reasonably acceptable when knowledge of their origin is suppressed.

> The same odor believed to come from strong cheese is much more tolerable than if thought to emanate from feces or rank feet.
>
> (Miller 1997: 247)

Disgust, partly because it is so violent and so instantaneous, appears natural, biological. Yet Darwin's and the native's disgust is instantaneous because they are immersed in their specific ethoses, which have attached intense passions to specific food regimes (its preparation and handling). Both Darwin and the 'native' are constituted by their ethological specificity. (The question of whether Darwin's disgust would have been provoked by a white man or woman touching his food is an open question.) What Darwin and the native of Tierra del Fuego are involved in is schismogenesis, a clash of different ethoses; two bodily regimes coming close together and shuddering back into their respective and newly intensified differences. Bateson's work on schismogenesis is pretty bleak with regards to the possibilities of acculturation or even cultural interchange more generally. Clearly, though, he captures something of the passionate intensity that can occur when cultures meet.

A novel that is structured around cultural migration but one that gives a very different picture of cross cultural exchange is Timothy Mo's novel *Sour Sweet*. Mo, whose father was Chinese and whose mother was English grew up as a young child in Hong Kong and then moved to England when he was ten (Ho 2000). *Sour Sweet* recounts the tale of a Chinese family moving to London in the 1960s. In this story of migration there is very little cultural interchange between Chinese and Anglo-British culture: the father works at a Chinese restaurant and their friends are all part of the Chinese-British community. The main culture clash is between the father and the Chinese Triad gang that he gets embroiled with. Yet this sets the scene for a comical staging of cultural disgust that is I think worth noting.

Chen, the father, is persuaded to borrow money from a Triad gang and in the process becomes indebted to the gang in various ways the least of which is a financial debt. Chen is beside himself with worry and consequently can't concentrate at work:

> As he waited absent-mindedly on his tables, Chen worried at the problem. Quite naturally his concentration on immediate matters slipped. He began to confuse orders (bringing lurid orange sweet

and sour port with pineapple chunks to outraged Chinese customers and white, bloody chicken and yellow duck's feet to appalled Westerners), bumped into his colleagues in the swing-doors, and stared vacantly into the customers' eyes as they indicated with diminishing degrees of subtlety that they wished to pay their bills and leave.

(Mo 2003 [1982]: 66)

What is telling here is that this restaurant worked as a place of non-cultural contact; or rather this was a Chinese restaurant as a delicate balance of two Chinas. While one China looks outward to the white British clientele (a filtered version of China, reworked, recoded for Western consumption) the other China is a Chinese China, of transplanted customs, and practices. These two Chinas exist side by side until one is forced to look at the other; the Western customers to look at the Chinese food that would be eaten by Chinese and the Chinese clientele are forced to recognise what China has become as a migration. Usually in the restaurant schismogenesis is mitigated and managed to the point of an implicit ethological stand off. It is only when the management falls apart that the cultural scene turns to mutual disgust. Schismogenesis seems best to be seen in an initial encounter of cultural difference: the global success of Chinese cuisine, as well as the importance of Chinese restaurants for Chinese diasporas around the world-suggests more varied possibilities of acculturation and the management of schismogenesis.

ORWELL'S SHAME

At the same time as Gregory Bateson was undertaking fieldwork amongst the Iatmul people in New Guinea, and while he was writing about schismogenesis and ethos back in Cambridge, the journalist and novelist George Orwell was undertaking his own empirical study of schismogenesis. In the late 1920s and early 1930s in London and Paris, and again in 1936 in the industrial towns of Yorkshire and Lancashire, Orwell plunged himself into a world of poverty and dirt. The books of this period *Down and Out in Paris and London* and *The Road to Wigan Pier* were experiments in the limits and possibilities of ethos. To write these books meant sleeping rough in London, working in terrible cafés in Paris and living in dirty lodgings in Wigan. While *Down and Out in Paris and London* (1933) was provoked by Orwell's own poverty, *The Road to Wigan Pier* (1937) was commissioned by a publisher. Yet in some ways both books and the experiences that they retold were a response to his passionate self-criticism.

Orwell returned to England after working for five years as a colonial police officer in Burma. He returns shameful of the despotism he has willingly taken part in, haunted by, 'Innumerable remembered faces – faces of prisoners in the dock, of men waiting in the condemned cells, or subordinates I had bullied and aged peasants I had snubbed, of servants and coolies I had hit with my fist in moments of rage' (Orwell 1975 [1937]: 129). Orwell recognises himself as divided between ethos (which was thoroughly bound by class) and what Bateson called 'eidos' – the rational, logical reasoning self (which was thoroughly convinced by socialism). In his own words he was 'both a snob and a revolutionary'. *The Road to Wigan Pier* is directed at the realisation that rational argument misunderstands the hold that ethos has over each and every one of us. In describing the extensiveness of his own class ethos Orwell sees it as determining the very way he moves his body:

> It is easy for me to say that I want to get rid of class-distinctions, but nearly everything I think and do is a result of class-distinctions. All my notions – notions of good and evil, of pleasant and unpleasant, of funny and serious, of ugly and beautiful – are essentially middle-class notions; my taste in books and food and clothes, my sense of honour, my table manners, my turns of speech, my accent, even the characteristic movements of my body, are the products of a special kind of upbringing and a special niche about half-way up the social hierarchy.
>
> (Orwell 1975 [1937]: 114)

The experiments in rough living are undertaken because Orwell is faced with the evidence of class schismogenesis even (perhaps especially) amongst those who rationally want to see the end of class divisions. *The Road to Wigan Pier* is an odd and uncomfortable read. For one thing the feeling of ethological schismogenesis is performed through the address of the text: the book is only addressed to those outside the working class. Similarly while Orwell is undertaking what might best be thought of as experiments in disgust, the reader is constantly being implicitly solicited on the matter of taste (this is disgusting, isn't it?) a solicitation which is designed to provoke the very reactions that he discusses as being so problematic for a progressive politics.

The mapping of ethos is undertaken along its contours and these contours have only one tone – revulsion. Reading across Orwell's writing, particularly his journalism and memoirs, you are faced with a figure that, not only finds revulsion in others, but is clearly compelled by self-disgust. His early life, especially his time at the boarding school that he attended from the age of eight to thirteen, taught him ethos through the deep pedagogy of shame and humiliation, and in this way, internalised feelings of self-disgust. His reminiscence 'Such, Such Were the Joys' (1947), begins with him being sent away to boarding school at the age of eight. Not uncommonly he starts to wet his bed at night. After a couple of bed wettings he is threatened with a beating. But rather than being told this by his headmaster he is told, unusually, by the headmaster's wife, who the children call 'Flip'. This is the scene in which he is being told of future punishments:

> 'Here is a little boy,' said Flip, indicating me to the strange lady, 'who wets his bed every night. Do you know what I am going to do if you wet your bed again?' she added turning to me. 'I am going to get the Sixth Form to beat you.'
> The strange lady put on an air of being inexpressibly shocked, and exclaimed 'I-should-*think*-so!'
>
> (Orwell 1947: 380)

He mishears 'Sixth Form' as Mrs Form and assumes that it is the other severe lady who is talking to him, who is going to beat him. Orwell's memory of this occasion is saturated by shame:

> To this day I can feel myself almost swooning with shame as I stood, a very small, round-faced boy in short corduroy knickers [short trousers], before the two women. I could not speak. I felt that I should die if 'Mrs Form' were to beat me. But my dominant feeling was not fear or even resentment: it was simply shame because one more person, and that a woman, had been told of my disgusting offence.
>
> (Orwell 1947: 380–1)

It is this pedagogy of shame and disgust that is such an elemental figure in Orwell's work and provides a more effective class investment than the mere ideological beliefs that are usually associated with social class:

> It may not greatly matter if the average middle-class person is brought up to believe that the working classes are ignorant, lazy, drunken, boorish, and dishonest; it is when he is brought up to believe that they are dirty that the harm is done. And in my childhood we were brought up to believe that they were dirty. Very early in life you acquired the idea that there was something subtly repulsive about a working-class body; you would not get nearer to it than you could help.
>
> (Orwell 1975 [1937]: 112)

This then might be both the starting point and conclusion of Orwell's 'disgust experiment'. In between is the work of encounter.

It becomes obvious that Orwell, in *The Road to Wigan Pier*, has not gone out to find an average working class Wigan family to lodge with. He has gone out to find an exceptionally disgusting family to lodge with: these are the Brookers. The Brookers run both a lodging house and a 'tripe shop'. The shop has dead flies in the window, and beetles crawling around the tripe. Tripe is the lining of a cow's stomach, it is cheap, nutritious, and notorious for its indigestible texture and the length of time required for cooking it. Mrs Brooker is monstrously overweight and confined to a sofa where she eats gargantuan meals and wipes her mouth with scraps of newspaper that she leaves lying around. Mr Brooker does most of the work, which includes serving the lodgers food with filthy hands (bread always comes with dark fingerprints on its surface). Chamber pots are always full, and remain under the kitchen table during meals. Both the Brookers complain incessantly, and their general bitterness adds to the disgust of the scene. Passion, sensorial experience, and perception congregate most particularly around Mr Brooker and his bitterness:

> In the mornings he sat by the fire with a tub of filthy water, peeling potatoes at the speed of a slow-motion picture. I never saw anyone who could peel potatoes with quite such an air of brooding resentment. You could see the hatred of this 'bloody woman's work', as he called it, fermenting inside him, a kind of bitter juice. He was one of those people who can chew their grievances like a cud.
>
> (Orwell 1975 [1937]: 11)

Bitterness is what feeds Mr Brooker, his sense of injustice, his spite (he chews it, like a cow). But it is also bitterness that seems to feed off Mr Brooker: at one point Orwell describes Mr Brooker's sense of injustice as a worm living in his bowels. Mr Brooker's potato peeling seems to infuse the food with bitterness (clearly all of the meals were indescribably revolting) and the sense of this work being an infringement of gender roles further intensifies the bitterness.

Orwell didn't need to stay with the Brookers. They are neither representative of the class that Orwell is looking at, nor of the lodgings available in Wigan. Orwell's disgust experiment is, in the end, aimed directly at himself. The bitterness that drives Mr Brooker mimes the bitterness that drives Orwell and is most evident when he is writing about his own childhood humiliations. What starts out as an investigation of complementary schismo-genesis (the intensifying of difference through class distinction) turns out to be symmetrical schismogenesis – where mutual bitterness is the affective ingredient that drives class division. Orwell's bitterness is, in the end, self-reflexive and it is that that proves the only possible way out of the stranglehold of his own ethos. To get there required a season in hell.

Passionate culture, or ethos, is learnt mostly as tacit knowledge, or tacit tuning. The pedagogic agents (the policing agents of ethos) are disdain and disgust, their affective actions are humiliation and shame. The positive values instilled in us as children are never as deeply embedded in us as those moments when we are caught in shame's humiliating embrace. Ethos is passionate culture internalised through the fear of such humiliations. Ethnological clashes can bring the passionate intensity of, and propensity towards, self-disgust to the surface. But (as I want to show in the next chapter) ethological clashes also have the power to dislodge the hold that shame has over us, to transform shame and humility into a liberating (rather than vainglorious) pride.

3 The Feeling of Structures

(On migration, memory, and the slaves' points of view)

In this chapter I start out from the idea that our 'feelings' (our passionate response to the world) are, to some degree, organised in advance by social structures (but rarely absolutely). We start by looking at Raymond Williams' suggestion that cultural analysts should examine the world of culture as a 'structure of feeling'. I want to augment this idea by suggesting that social structures are primarily uneven in their distribution and are, thereby, experienced (felt) unevenly. To explore this we look at instances of the history of colonial and postcolonial social structures. In this chapter we meet the Caribbean historian and thinker C. L. R. James and cultural theorist and historian Paul Gilroy. We look briefly at the literature of West Indian London and drop in on Cape Town's District Six, in South Africa.

The moment you are born your relationship with the state begins. Actually it began before that; it was waiting for you all along, preparing itself just for you. Your world was imagined and plotted in advance: with a web of care and distrust to throw over you; a network of control and containment; an itinerary of permissibility, possibility and prevention already in place. But it waited patiently; it needed to know who you were: would it need to turn-up the suspicion, concentrate on control rather than permissibility? It needed to see how you fitted into the structures of the social.

On a global level the unevenness of these structures are evident when you move from one nation state to another. Will you be treated as an 'economic migrant', a doubted refugee, a welcome visitor, a needed addition to a work-force, a valued tourist? Looking around international airports is always a chastening experience as wealthy business people head for first class lounges while other families travel with their home on their back; holiday makers make a beeline for the bar while young men and women clutch their parents in tearful goodbyes. The scared, the homesick, and the daunted offer a sobering comparison to the over-excited and the blasé. What will your passport entail: a friendly nonchalance or an invasive strip search? Social structures impinge on us and generate passionate responses: fear, anger, euphoria, anxiety. But passionate culture maintains a dynamic relationship to these social structures: it responds.

In 1961 the cultural historian and literary theorist Raymond Williams published *The Long Revolution* and with it developed a phrase (which he had coined back in 1954 in his *Preface to Film*) which deserves to sit at the centre of the study of passionate culture. The phrase, 'structures of feeling', is both hard and soft: it plays on the tough architectural motif of structure, softening it with the more fluid and immaterial moods of feeling. As Williams has it: 'it is as firm and definite as "structure" suggests, yet it operates in the most delicate and least tangible parts of our activity' (Williams 1992 [1961]: 48). For Williams the term 'structures of feelings' was his way of attending to cultural moments from the past as unfinished: culture in-process, in the midst of things. One of the deadening aspects of studying culture is to treat cultural objects and practices as complete and replete with meanings that will only require technical interpretation. Williams' work was an attempt to study the past as the living, breathing and partly inchoate traces of experience (of experience in the making). When he offers a definition of the term in his book *Marxism and Literature* he makes this explicit: 'For structure of feeling can be defined as social experience in solution as distinct from other social semantic functions which have been precipitated and are more evidently and more immediately available' (1977: 133–4).

The phrase then has these two elements that pull irritably at each other but also need each other: what would a feeling be like if it wasn't related to something bigger than itself; structures would remain abstractions if they didn't force a response from you, if they didn't touch you somehow. Williams had in mind structures such as 'the organization of production, the structure of the family, the structure of institutions which express or govern social relationships, the characteristic forms through which members of society communicate' (Williams 1992 [1961]: 42). The feelings he was interested in exploring consisted of the 'characteristic elements of impulse, restraint, and tone; specifically affective elements of consciousness and relationships: not feelings against thought, but thought as felt and feeling as thought: practical consciousness of a present kind, in a living relationship to continuity' (1977: 132).

The complexity of these elements as they are brought together (as they are in actuality) was what Williams was after, and it was related to his sense that culture was a 'whole way of life' (1992 [1961]: 40). Yet though this sense of wholeness rings with the suggestion of completion and evenness, Williams was careful to insist that structures of feeling are unevenly experienced: 'I do not mean that the structure of feeling, any more than the social character, is possessed in the same way by the many individuals in the community' (1992 [1961]: 48). It would be hard for a writer like Williams, growing up in the working class communities of the Welsh valleys, and then being educated as a scholarship-boy at Cambridge, not to see the evidence of unevenness at every turn. To study structures of feelings is an attempt to find patterns across culture, and there is no reason why these patterns can't be jagged and conflictual, rather than smooth and symmetrical.

Nonetheless there is a sense that 'structures of feeling' seem to map culture as a form of coherence (or emergent coherence), and if not a unity, then a centrally shared world of experience. In this, structures of feeling, are most clearly seen for Williams as the overriding feeling of a generation (the sense of tired optimism that seems to come through certain postwar artworks in the 1950s, for instance) or of a national culture. It is hard to think how the phrase might be usefully extended to the much more intransigent differences of multicultural experiences and conflict, for instance. Would Williams understand the encounters between a group of refugees and a group from a host culture as constituting two separate structures of feeling? How would, in Apartheid South Africa, for instance, the structure of feelings of black township dwellers, connect to the ways of thinking, feeling and living of the white elites? Would the structure of Apartheid be their main commonality (their only 'whole way of life'), and wouldn't this be, essentially, a completely different state of feeling for these two communities?

One way of getting Williams' intuitions to work for the study of passionate culture in a more global setting, in a setting that wants to register the comings and goings of both conquerors and conquered, is to reverse its ordering. Rather than structures of feelings it would mean looking at the feelings of structures (feelings of difference in relation to social structures). Here both feelings and structures might work more autonomously and perhaps more precariously: a social structure that might seem to dominate specific life experiences (the organisation of a social world along classist and racist lines, for instance) may sit alongside any number of feelings, only some of which relate directly to this structure (though the indirect affects might be much more ubiquitous). Some of the most badly treated people of recent history might have good reason to see the structure of the state as saturating their lives. The Australian report *Bringing them Home: Report of the National Inquiry into the Separation of Aboriginal and Torres Strait Islander Children from Their Families* is made up, in part, of the testimonies of Aborigines and Torres Strait Islanders who were forcibly removed from their families during the middle decades of the twentieth century. They tell the abysmal stories of the 'stolen generations'. The second testimony in the report states: 'Our life pattern was created by the government policies and are forever with me, as though an invisible anchor around my neck' (confidential submission 338, Human Rights and Equal Opportunities Commission 1997: non-paginated). We will come back to this report in chapter six: and we will see alongside this invisible structural anchor, the passionate determinism and resilience of these people of the stolen generations.

In what follows I want to pursue this sense of social entanglement: where social structures generate passionate responses but don't necessarily saturate or exhaust passionate culture. I want to see what happens when the passionate culture of social structures is looked at in the crossings and networks of colonial conquest, migration and multiculturalism. In all these examples social structures might be both the target of feelings as well as the generator of feelings. But it might also become apparent that things are happening in what we might think of as the shadows of social structures, in the places where structures are more improvisational, more antagonised, and fundamentally less controlling.

FROM THE SLAVES' POINTS OF VIEW

If the structures we live across are complex, contradictory and desperately uneven, then the perspective we see them from matters. A lord and a labourer will, of course, feel the uneven and unequal social structures unevenly and unequally: the structures are simply designed that way. Accounts of culture are positioned to show us social structures seen from certain perspectives, with the result that they necessarily obscure and obliterate other perspectives. In Paul Gilroy's brilliant book, *The Black Atlantic*, he offers a challenge and an opportunity: 'the time has come for the primary history of modernity to be reconstructed from the slaves' points of view' (Gilroy 1993: 55).

The point of Gilroy's work, and in this he is following the example set by C. L. R. James (whom he acknowledges), is to pursue history from the slaves' perspective but not in the belief that we need to fill in all the missing gaps of history. Seeing history from the slaves' points of view won't just fill out the historical record a bit by adding another layer to its thickening complexity. Rather it will re-orchestrate it, give us a different account of the modern and a more thorough and more critical perspective with which to view it. Simply put, the wager is that the slaves' perspective will make for better, more expansive, history telling. There are a number of reasons for this. Slavery in its essence was trans-national involving the complex crossings of what Gilroy refers to as the black Atlantic. Here the task is to shift from a perspective tied to nation states to one that works in the crossings between and over nation states. Thus the Atlantic offers Gilroy a complex unit of analysis that is crucially not limited to national experiences: 'I want to develop the suggestion that cultural historians could take the Atlantic as one single, complex unit of analysis in their discussions of the modern world and use it to produce an explicitly transnational and intercultural perspective' (Gilroy 1993: 15). This is not, I would add, to suggest an overarching global perspective, but one that is attuned to the movements of people that are always concrete and always entangled within the pull of nation.

The Atlantic, for Gilroy, provides an opportunity for finding patterns to culture (in a way not too dissimilar to Williams' project), yet while Williams wants to find the patterns of common feeling of a group, class, or nation at a particular time, Gilroy's sense of patterning is more complex and has, fundamentally, more reach. Gilroy describes the Atlantic patterning as 'fractal'. In fractal geometry, fractal shapes appear to be complex and arbitrary (in the sense that they are not squares and circles, etc.) and can expand infinitely while maintaining the same shape. Similarly a shard of a fractal contains within it the blueprint of the whole structure. Gilroy explains his use of the term fractal in the following way: 'I am thinking of fractal geometry as an analogy here because it allows for the possibility that a line of infinite length can enclose a finite area. The opposition between totality and infinity is thus recast in a striking image of the scope for agency in restricted conditions' (Gilroy 1993: 236–7). A fractal might involved a concentration on a singular event (of criss-crossing routes) but it will never be 'individual' (in that strong sense of pertaining to the self as progenitor of meaning and passion). Fractals always (potentially) connect, even in isolation.

To make this patterning more concrete it is worth taking a closer look at one of the examples that Gilroy gives. Much of his book is concerned with the Atlantic presence in Britain and America through the movements of musicians and music. Gilroy follows the Atlantic crossings that made Jimi Hendrix's British triumph possible, or enabled the coolly-effervescent dance music of Soul II Soul in the 1980s. His account of these musical crossings and crossovers begins in the 1870s when the Fisk Jubilee Singers toured England, Ireland, Wales and Scotland. Fisk University is in Nashville and was established 1867 to provide education for former slaves and their offsprings; the Jubilee Singers sang spirituals ('John Brown's Body', 'Sing Low, Sweet Chariot', and so on) from the days of slavery, and were an enormous success spawning a number of other gospel choirs who travelled Europe and South Africa in the 1870s. Gilroy traces the fractal lines of influence and confluence as the songs travel across the Atlantic and back again, gaining in authority and in authenticity. Authenticity is usefully queried here, and any simple bonding of authenticity to a sense of origin is rejected in favour of a more nuanced sense of authenticity as a production, and in this case a production of movement and memory. It matters little whether or not the Fisk Singers performed their repertoire in the actual style and manner in which former slaves sang it. Authority and authenticity are gained precisely because they are singing the slave songs and refusing the obnoxious buffoonery of minstrel and 'blackface' entertainment (white entertainers corked-up to look black).

The Jubilee Singers sang to royalty (to Queen Victoria and the Prince of Wales), to politicians (to William Gladstone) and to mass audiences of working class whites. They were routinely refused places to stay on account of their skin-colour, but were enthusiastically greeted and applauded by the various audiences that saw them, who recognised them as the true sound of the slaves' perspective and the very embodiment of the abolitionist ethos. As Gilroy claims, 'the Fisk Singers constructed an aura of seriousness around their activities and projected the memory of slavery outwards as the means to make their musical performances intelligible and pleasurable' (Gilroy 1993: 89). Thus the authenticity of their sound was linked to the histories of the Atlantic crossings that they brought to the music. And Gilroy's fractal movements is no simple one-way movement of black America to the imperial heartland: the experience of movement works its way back as the singers return to the US and influence the likes of W. E. B. Du Bois. For Gilroy the Jubilee singers and their range of productions (concerts and the varied publications that they produced to accompany the concerts) 'is especially important for anyone seeking to locate the origins of the polyphonic montage technique developed by Du Bois in *The Souls of Black Folk*' (Gilroy 1993: 89).

The most important precursor to Gilroy's work of writing culture from 'the slaves' points of view' is undoubtedly the work of the Trinidadian intellectual C. L. R. James. In the early 1930s James came to England (also spending time in France) and started work on his landmark history of the Haitian slave revolt (or San Domingo, as it was called during the colonial period), *The Black Jacobins: Toussaint L'Ouverture and the San Domingo Revolution*. James wrote the book at a time of intense Caribbean political unrest when there was constant discussion about the possibilities of independence for Trinidad and elsewhere in the region. The book tells the story of the Haitian slave revolts. In it James conjoins political history (the story of the causes and activities of the revolution) with cultural history. While his narrative is dedicated to the story

43

of the revolution he also pays particular attention to the social structures of slave life, in particular the pervasive differentiation ('divide and conquer') that is the constant theme of colonial rule. The strange 'logic' of colonial racism includes what looks like a metric way of measuring 'race' and the bizarre absoluteness of its implementation. James writes of the way that an intermediary social group emerged in San Domingo as a sort of managerial but subservient class. These were often the offspring of slaves and white colonials (usually of low rank). They fell under different social structures: for instance they were neither properly slaves nor free men and women, but had a small degree of relative autonomy to accrue wealth (although no voting rights). When this group began to prosper the colonial logic worked to block it:

> As they began to establish themselves, the jealousy and envy of the white colonists were transformed into ferocious hatred and fear. They divided the offspring of white and black and intermediate shades into 128 divisions. The true Mulatto was the child of the pure black and the pure white. The child of white and the Mulatto woman was a quarteron with ninety-six parts white and thirty-two parts black. But the quarteron could be produced by the white and the marabou in the proportion of 88 to 40, or by the white and the sacatra, in the proportion of 72 to 56 and so on all through the 128 varieties. But the sang-mêlé with 127 white parts and one black part was still a man of colour.
>
> (James 2001 [1938]: 31)

The absurdity of this 'system' was evident in its final verdict (either you're white or you're not). For James this is not evidence of the sophistication of the social technology of colonialism, but a clear sign of the lengths it would go to protect its (financial) interests. Instead of an illogical rationalism, what we have is a blunt instrument of financial self-interest and a broad strategy of attempting to defeat opposition through division.

For both James and Gilroy the 'slaves' point of view' (and the perspective of the slaves' progeny) wouldn't offer a counter history to the story of the modern; it would be that story. What is unique in the slaves' perspective is the constant modernity of the slaves' position:

> The sugar plantation has been the most civilising as well as the most demoralising influence in West Indian development. When three centuries ago the slaves came to the West Indies, they entered directly into the large-scale agriculture of the sugar plantation,

which was a modern system. It further required the slaves live together in a social relation far closer than any proletariat of the time.

The cane when reaped had to be rapidly transported to what was factory production. The product was shipped abroad for sale. Even the cloth the slaves wore and the food they ate was imported. The Negroes, therefore, from the very start lived a life that was in its essence a modern life. That is their history – as far as I have been able to discover, a unique history.

(James 1962: 296–7)

To tell history from the slaves' perspective necessitates recognising the centrality of this modernity rather than seeing the black Atlantic crossings as peripheral to such an account.

What James and Gilroy do is re-code more familiar stories of the modernising impulse told as a tale of discovery, conquest and production. From the 'slaves' points of view', colonial rule stumbles to adjust to the modernity that they have embroiled themselves and others in. The stakes are high: and the main stake is in articulating a sense of agency within history. Who is it then who is making modern history: the slave or his or her master? By re-coding this history to see the agency in the slaves' stories (in the revolutionary figure of Toussaint L'Ouverture and all those that joined the revolution, for James; or in the Atlantic artists, musicians, and writers, for Gilroy) the representation of 'world-historical-figures' shift:

> Thus James does not represent Caribbean people as an old African people, a traditional people, decimated by plantation slavery and the experience of forced migration, free – when abolition arrived – to go back to the old ways. James understood well enough that the history of modernity revolutionizes *everything*. Nothing could be turned back. Everything is transformed. Thus the people of the Caribbean – fortuitously, paradoxically – had been transformed into a kind of prototypical, modern people, no longer rooted in a traditional, religious or particularistic way of understanding the world. They had had – James argued – their own traditions transformed, fractured and violently inserted into the most advanced ideas of the time, into the very syntax of the declaration of the rights of man and into the dawn of a new world.
>
> (Hall 1998: 23)

And in this way the social structures that impinge on the slave (the bizarre metrics of race, or the day-to-day racism facing the Jubilee

Singers) is not simply responded to with a range of feelings (hurt, for instance, or rage), but is also countered with other structures, that bring other feelings into their orbit: the serious euphoria of the spirituals; the eventual dignity of national independence.

IS LIKE NOTHING

The dominant feeling of emigrants coming from the various parts of the British Commonwealth to Britain is not hard to hear: it is the tone of disappointment. But it is a complex disappointment, one that is syncopated by both exuberance and melancholia. If, for many emigrants, disappointment arose (from the lack of welcome they received on arrival) as soon as they disembarked from the ships that carried them from Trinidad, Barbados, Jamaica, from the subcontinent and elsewhere, other cultural structures emerged that demonstrated not just cultural resilience in the face of the constant racism of Britain, but a fierce social creativity that seemed to find energy from those mean possibilities, those dingy circumstances.

Samuel Selvon, an Indo-Caribbean Trinidadian, came to London in 1950. In an autobiographical essay Selvon talks about the way that he was creolised in Trinidad; less interested in sticking close to his Indian heritage he eagerly embraced black Trinidadian and American culture, alongside Hindi culture:

> I think I can say without question that this creolising process was the experience of a great many of my generation. It was so effective that one even felt a certain embarrassment and uneasiness on visiting a friend in whose household Indian habits and customs were maintained, as if it were a social stigma not to be western-ised. The roti and goat-curry was welcome, but why did they have to play Indian music instead of putting on a calypso or one of the American tunes from the hit parade.
>
> (Selvon 1979: 15–16)

In Trinidad he 'was one of the boys, doing my jump-up at Carnival time, giving and taking picong, liming for a freeness, drinking coconut water around the Savannah or eating a late-night roti down St. James' (15). In London, Selvon mixed with emigrants from various countries within the commonwealth, from the various islands that make up the Caribbean (referred to at the times as the West Indies) and from the subcontinent.

For British whites there were simply Jamaicans and Indians and the British ignorance of the Caribbean was for Selvon, astonishing, and in a strange way, uplifting:

> As far as the English were concerned, we were all one kettle of fish and classified as Jamaicans. Their ignorance of the Caribbean was astonishing. You can imagine, after being brought up to believe that Britain was the fountainhead of knowledge and learning, how staggered I was to be asked if we lived in trees, or if there were lions and tigers in my part of the world. Their ignorance engendered a feeling of pride in my own country.
>
> (Selvon 1979: 17)

Selvon's remarks are worth holding on to. Again we have a system of daily racism underwritten by the imposition of colonial superiority that, while it has a number of desolate material consequences (the everyday difficulty of finding work, food, lodgings), is never characterised by sophistication or nuance. Here, it is the dumb face of ignorance. More evidently racist activities are pictured as the brute face of stupidity. But what is also crucial here is that this social structure of daily ignorance and oppression gives rise to a feeling that might be hard to predict: pride and confidence. This is the feeling that Stuart Hall notices when he describes the benighted streets of London peppered with young black men and women who look confident, at home, in charge (Hall 1987).

In his 1956 novel *The Lonely Londoners*, Selvon chronicles the lives of a loose confederacy of arrivals (mostly men) from Trinidad, Barbados, Jamaica and other islands of the West Indies. The novel is written with a constant alternation between a West Indian vernacular (the creolised patois of West Indian English) and the more formal written language of British 'educated' English. Something of the swaying between the vernacular and the officially recognised English mirrors the various social structures that the arrivals live within and across. The character Moses is an old hand, having lived in London for a few years. His informal role is to initially look after the newer arrivals, find them lodgings, get them registered at the employment exchange and help them find work. Henry Oliver, known by his nickname as Sir Galahad, is one such new arrival from Trinidad. *The Lonely Londoners* weaves together the tales of Sir Galahad with those of other emigrants, and loosely holds these threads together through the figure of Moses. Sir Galahad faces the official structures of the state in the form of the limitations on the amount of money he could bring to the country and through his registering with the employment exchange, but most of the stories happen within other social structures that the emigrants have concocted for themselves: the convivial networks of friendships, and so on. For most of the novel the presence of the State is like a blunt antagonist that disallows them the possibility of prosperity or easy living. The feelings that circulate, the highs and lows of spirit are animated to a degree by the dominant social structures, but only to a degree; they constitute only one element within the narrative. For the most part West Indians mix with each other, talk to one another and hang out together.

Like all commonwealth citizens Selvon knew more about London and Britain than the majority of white Britons knew about the Caribbean. To come to London was to come to a place already know, already imagined, already fantasised. The second disappointment, but one that has a range of effects is the realisation that this imagined, Imperial London might well exist, but that it exists as a social structure at a distance. Emigration as a black or 'East Indian' within the structures of international racism always alters the condition of emigration. But if this experience is to be marginalised within the metropolitan imperial centres, it also gives the migrant a perspective that sees through the bluster and pomp of empire. Thus the experience of commonwealth emigration could also be an experience of an enlightenment, a recognition of the hollowness at the heart of empire. This is Moses talking to Sir Galahad:

> All them places is like nothing to me now. Is like when you back home and you hear fellars talk about Times Square and Fifth Avenue, and Charing Cross and gay Paree. You say to yourself, "Lord, them places must be sharp." Then you get a chance and you see them for yourself, and is like nothing.
>
> (Selvon 2006 [1956]: 73)

The year that Selvon published his novel, the writer Mike Philips emigrated from Guyana (called British Guyana when Philips emigrated). His experience of London resonates with a host of others. Describing his first years in London Philips writes:

> The operations of the state were accompanied by an imagery intended to transform the distant imperium into a routine aspect of our domestic imagination. London lurked in our language like a virus, carried on a stream of words and ideas which acquired the power of myth, and I had always possessed a mental map of the city which sketched out an outline of these institutions – Buckingham Palace. The British Museum. The LSE. The MCC. Parliament. The Foreign Office. Scotland Yard. [...] All these were landmarks in the London I knew before I set foot in its streets, but during my initial encounter with the city, they might as well have been operating on the moon. The London I lived in seemed to have a different history, and to be organised around different elements.
>
> (Phillips 2001: 30)

Philips, interestingly, describes a process which might be called the 'colonisation of the imagination', but the actuality of the imperial metropolis, the day-to-day reality of it, is sluggish bureaucracy, cold weather, ignorant racism. And while this disappoints it also works to deflate the imperial power that sets out to describe itself as the truth, the way, the light. This mixture of disappointment and enlightenment affects a range of critical insights. For instance, the day-to-day racism that Sir Galahad experiences allows him to see a certain abstraction in the business of racist perception. In one scene Galahad is talking to his blackness: 'So Galahad talking to the colour Black, as if is a person, telling it that is not *he* who causing botheration in the place, but Black, who is a worthless thing for making trouble all about' (Selvon 2006 [1956]: 77).

You'd be hard-pressed not to hear the anger and melancholy in the emigrant experience and the slaves' perspectives. In these accounts the suffering in the face of antagonistic social structures is immediate, material. But I also think that it would be equally hard not to hear the exuberance, the pride, the creative defiance which these narratives also articulate. For Jean Rhys' a white West Indian, who emigrated from Dominica to England in 1906, emigration alters everything, but most specifically it alters feeling. In her novel *Voyage in the Dark* (1934), for instance, she describes an arrival to an elsewhere:

> It was as if a curtain had fallen, hiding everything I had ever known. It was almost like being born again. The colours were different,

the smells different, the feeling things gave you right down inside yourself was different. Not just the difference between heat; light; darkness; grey. But a difference in the way I was frightened and the way I was happy...

(Rhys cited in Nasta 2002: 63)

Feelings change, and the structures of the social change too: how one maps onto the other is the question facing anyone wanting to study passionate culture, especially the passions of modernity seen from the slaves' points of view.

DISTRICT SIX, CAPE TOWN 1867–1982

The story of District Six, an area of Cape Town, South Africa, offers a materially visceral example of the some of the ways that social structures and passionate culture (structures and feelings) connect and disconnect. The history of District Six during the second half of the twentieth century is, of course, inescapably determined by the structuring agency of South Africa's Apartheid regime (established from 1948). If the Apartheid regime instituted racial (and racist) legislation that divided the people of South Africa into three categories of 'Whites', 'Coloureds' and 'Blacks' (with some subcategories operating within these larger ones) then the actuality of District Six was a forceful reminder of the infinitely more complex history of the various diasporas that have, since the fifteenth century, congregated (either through forced or willing migration) in Cape Town.

From the 'slaves' point of view' Cape Town is not 'white', 'coloured' and 'black', but the outcome of European colonisation (by the Dutch, British, and Portuguese); of the decimation of indigenous populations (Khoekhoe and San); of the forced migrations of slaves and indentured labourers (often coercively indentured) coming to South Africa from Angola, West Africa, Bengal, Madras, Mauritius, Madagascar, Java, Indonesia, Malaysia and elsewhere; of the migration of East European refugees; and so on. Cape Town is the result of the mixing and separating of cultures, of lives, as these populations became 'South African'. In 1950 Apartheid (the Afrikaans word means separateness) sought to establish an emphatic segregated geography through the combination of the Population

Registration Act (which instituted the tripartite racial classifi-
cations for all South Africans) and the Group Areas Act (which
sought to establish distinct racial 'zones'). In 1966 District Six was
declared a whites-only group area, and between 1966 and 1984
60,000 people were forcibly removed and their homes razed to the
ground (McEachern 1998). The social structure of the Apartheid
regime obliterated a community.

District Six had suffered racist divisiveness before (black South
Africans were removed in 1901, but small numbers moved back
into the District in the decades that followed [see Ngcelwane 1998
on this]) and had become, within the racial structures of Apartheid, a mainly 'coloured' area. But the diversity of what such a
term might mean proved the lie of Apartheid. From the mid nineteenth century through to its final demolition in 1984, District Six
was home to Hindus, Jews, Christians, Muslims; to Lithuanians
and Chinese; to shopkeepers, factory workers and petty criminals.
In a whole host of memoirs and novels District Six is remembered
as a vibrant community where children grew up unaware of skin
colour, where white and non-white played together, where sexual,
ethnic and religious differences were accepted in a way that was an
anathema within the Apartheid imagination. Rozena Maart's
Rosa's District 6 (2004), Richard Rive's *Buckingham Palace,
District Six* (1987), Nomvuyo Ngcelwane's *Sala Kahle District Six:
An African Woman's Perspective* (1998) and Linda Fortune's *The
House in Tyne Street: Childhood Memories of District Six* (1996)
paint a picture of a community where poverty and generosity,
rivalry and loyalty sit side by side. This is far
from being a utopia (Rozena Maart, for instance, writes about the
informal social hierarchies that orchestrated the district) but as
an example of actually existing 'multiculturalism' it provided a
concrete critique of Apartheid racism.

When the bulldozers moved in 'everyone in the District died a little'
(Rive 1987: 117): social structures had conquered cosmopolitan
community. The cleared District was renamed Zonnebloem and
a whites-only Technikon (technical college) was opened along with
accommodation for Afrikaans-speaking government employees.
The transnational corporation BP began to plan a large scale
redevelopment of the area. Out of the rubble of defeat the former
residents of District Six came together to form the 'Hands Off

51

District Six Committee' and declared the area 'salted earth' (a reference to the ancient practices of salting the earth to make it useless for cultivation) until Apartheid ended. The protest movement effectively blocked BP's or any other development of the District.

When Apartheid finally fell in 1994 the committee organised a memorial exhibition in a former Methodist Church (one of the few buildings remaining from before the demolition). The 'temporary' exhibition became a museum (www.districtsix.co.za) dedicated to remembering District Six and memorialising the plight of all forcibly displaced people. The intention of the museum is to place memory in the service of a political remembering and restitution:

> In 1966 District Six was declared a white group area. Shortly afterwards the first bulldozers moved in and set about destroying homes in which generations of families had lived. Intent on erasing District Six from the map of Cape Town the Apartheid State attempted to redesign the space of District Six, renaming it Zonnebloem. Today, only the scars of the removals remain. In this exhibition we do not wish to recreate District Six as much as to re-possess the history of the area as a place where people lived, loved and struggled. It is an attempt to take back our right to signpost our lives with those things we hold dear.
>
> (District Six Museum cited in McEachern 1998: 504)

As such the museum is a continuation of the struggle. As Dipesh Chakrabarty puts it 'the museum developed into a site of communal memory, not a nostalgic monument to a dead past but a living memory that is part of the struggle against racism in post-Apartheid South Africa' (Chakrabarty 2002: 10).

The museum is a collective enterprise where former residents have donated memory material (photographs, recollections, and so on) and time (the volunteers will take you on guided tours of the desolated area pointing out the spectral remains of what is no longer there). It is a monument to the brutality of a social structure and to the passions of those that resisted it:

> Remember District 6. Remember the racism which took away our homes and our livelihood and which sought to steal away our humanity. Remember also our will to live, to hold fast to that

Figure 3.1 District Six Museum interior 2007. Photograph by Paul Grendon and with kind permission of the District Six Museum; copyright Paul Grendon and the District Six Museum.

which marks us as human beings: our generosity, our love of justice, and our care for each other.

(District Six Museum cited in Coombes 2003: 121)

Such passionate culture stakes out a politics of hope based on the conviction of remaining 'unreconciled to the past and unconsoled by the present' (Parry 2004). It is a passionate politics striving towards a future that will be forever cognisant of the brutality that gave birth to it.

The slaves' perspective is a position that is dedicated to resisting the amnesia of the present. Its role in mapping passionate culture is central: it marks not just the hatreds and fears that characterise too much history of the modern, but also the hopes and desires of the passions that have struggled to find a path away from hatred and fear. If the only thing strong enough to block passion is passion (as Hume and so many others thought), then the politics of hope needs to look to the slave's points of view for the passionate politics of generosity and care.

The passionate history of the modern not only includes the passions of groups towards groups, of people towards people, it has also been mediated in substantial ways by a passion towards things. No history of the present could possible ignore the 'governance of the commodity' and the passions that animate our relationship to things. To move from the slaves' perspectives to the luxurious world of things is to remember that the history of the modern has been primarily dictated by a desire for gain. That desire has mobilised, in spectacular and spectral ways, the lure of things.

4 The Lure of Things

(On commodities, display, and sensual transformation)

In this chapter we meet desirable commodities: shiny new things, expensive trinkets, unnecessary luxuries as well as ordinary things. The world of the commodity is an essential part of passionate culture; the empire of the commodity sets out to seduce us, to make our hearts beat faster, to make us envious creatures. To show passionate things we first visit the World's Fair before stopping off (if only briefly) in the domain of advertising. But we also spend a little time with the afterlife of the commodity – its homely life, and the passionate attachments it can foster. For this journey the German critic Walter Benjamin will be our tour guide.

LUST AND LUSTRE

How does the world of commodities persuade us that we want them, that we need them? How is it that this absurdly expensive designer handbag will become this month's must-have accessory? Why do I lust over a mobile phone with a touch-control screen and a sleek, mirror-black casing? Why does that car look so gorgeous? Why should I smell of this specific aftershave; what will happen if I just smell of me? Why should I be persuaded by Nike to 'just do it' (and what is it that I should just do)? Why would I want a flat-screen TV, a black chenille cardigan, an iPod? Why must your legs show no signs of hair? Why should I wear those clothes when these are so comfortable, so friendly? Why should I put myself in hock to the demands of the empire of the commodity? And why am I so willing to submit?

The answers to these questions are partly provided by the public relations arm of commodity culture: advertising. New things very rarely go out in public alone, naked. For the most part they are surrounded by a fanfare trumpeting their special qualities; the differences that they will make to your life; the benefits that you will receive. This aftershave will have women throwing themselves at you (and without it you will be lonely, smelly, unloved). This car is an aerodynamic miracle that will drive you to the wildest mountain roads, just to give you the pleasure of its quiet engine and smooth suspension. This mobile phone will turn your world into a soft, spongy place where you can float from one friend to the next. Your legs will look like forests of cacti without this new scientifically-improved hair-removal cream.

I see a flat screen TV and I become an eager supplicant at the altar of commercial culture. Am I, therefore, simply lured and lulled into a hypnotized dream-world by this promotional culture? Have I no will-power, or more importantly, no critical faculties that might be able to resist this lure? Can't I tune my scepticism to the fanfare that is declaring that my life will be changed forever when I get this TV and that, from then on, any film will seem like a roller-coaster ride of sensual abandon? We make a mistake, I think, if we see commodities as 'all smoke and mirrors', as simply a con-trick that fools us into believing the improbable claims of promotional culture. Most importantly we fail to see this commodified world as passionate culture if we see it simply as persuasion (in the sense of convincing us of its version of the world). Commodity culture doesn't address us as rational beings (if it did who in the world would buy half the things we do) it addresses us as passionate sensualists, as willing or unwilling hedonists. And it does so not simply through the world of advertising but through the fashioned object itself. And here it is crucial that we see the empire of the commodity as animated by the lustre of fashion.

Walter Benjamin wrote that 'Fashion stands in opposition to the organic. It couples the living body to the inorganic world' (Benjamin 1999: 8). Of course in 1935, when he wrote this, the word organic didn't have that same meaning as it does in our environmentally-minded times; here organic refers to the realm of living, creaturely beings, rather than the world of things. Benjamin is noting that it is fashion's (and advertising's) role to conjoin the human creaturely world to the world of things. He carries on by offering us one of the most evocative phrases for understanding the lure of commodity culture: 'the fetishism that succumbs to the sex appeal of the inorganic is its [fashion's] vital nerve' (8). 'The sex appeal of the inorganic' suggests at least two things: one is that the desires that commodities solicit are of an intensity equal to and overlapping with sexual desire; the second is that this sex appeal is a characteristic, not simply overlaying commodity culture, but as a property of the commodified 'thing'. And don't we lust over objects in a similar way to the way we lust over bodies: aren't we attracted to their curves, their tautness, their sheen, their smoothness, the sounds they make, how they feel against your skin, how they look and taste?

Like the world of sexual attraction and the social norms of beauty, the 'sex appeal of the inorganic' is dynamic and changes over time. This is what makes fashion such a historical force. But if human sex appeal sometimes relies on artifice and intensive fashioning (from cosmetic surgery to gym routines) the sex appeal of the commodity must rely entirely on artifice (after all, the commodity is always artificial to the extent that it is a manufactured thing). Such artifice is a quality of the commodity, it provides its lustre and it demands our lust. The question that needs both asking and answering is 'how does it do this'? What are the tricks, the cosmetic practices of the commodity that can make the world of things so attractive? In this chapter I want to argue that it is the sensual aspect of the commodity that is designed to solicit our acquiescence, and that the world of commodities doesn't just supply 'things that are nice to touch', but is in the business of making magic, of producing things that have undergone sensual transformations and adjustments. Heavy things appear light; kitchen units seem to hover off the floor; doors that you should be able to slam shut just seem to float their way home and finish with a satisfying click. To get a sense of the sensual work that things do and how they fit into a world of passionate culture, we need to follow Benjamin's exploration of commodity culture.

For Benjamin, one crucial site for examining commodity culture is World's Fairs and International exhibitions. His claim is that 'world exhibitions are places of pilgrimage to the commodity fetish' (1999: 7). So far in this book we have been looking at passionate culture (ethos) as a space of sentimental and sensual training: a pedagogy of the passions. In Benjamin's writing (and elsewhere) world exhibitions take centre stage as the place where commodities circulate with 'their gloves off', so to speak, where their passionate performance is at its most intense, where things come together in a display of international rivalry and thingly solidarity. World exhibitions (and promotional culture in general) provides us with lessons in desire, where we can gawk and gape at effervescent objects and yearn (and learn) to posses them.

RADIANT THINGS

World exhibitions are an amalgam of the classroom, the department store, and the carnival, with a heavy sprinkling of religion, and orchestrated by national loyalties and rivalries. The world exhibition is Coney Island, Canterbury Cathedral, and Macy's combined; a synthesis of Disney World and the Musée du Louvre; the Taj Mahal coupled with Billingsgate. The origin of trade fairs takes us back to ancient times, to Egypt, India, China, Mexico, Greece and Rome. In the last thousand years of history, commercial fairs were part and parcel of the way business got done. But in the modern period such cultural forms were both distilled and expanded, and paraded as educational entertainment (rather than simply commercial necessity). The modern exhibitions showed the latest machinery, the most contemporary scientific processes, and the most up-to-date goods. In the twentieth century (especially in the first half) they included big wheels, big dippers, striptease, museums, industrial machinery, scientific demonstrations, colonial acquisitions (with displays of 'native' peoples) and an almost utopian sense of a endless plenitude of things. In the nineteenth century there were international exhibitions in Chile, Peru, Argentina, China, Japan, Vienna, Ireland, Italy, South Africa, Britain, France, United States of America and Australia. A list of the most famous fairs would include the Great Exhibition of 1851, the *Exposition Universelle* (Paris) of 1867, the 1893 World's Columbian Exposition (also called the Chicago World's Fair), the 1933–34 Chicago Century of Progress International Exposition, the 1939–40 New York World's Fair, the 1964–5 New York World's Fair, and Expo '70 in, Osaka, Japan. Expo 2010 takes place in Shanghai, China.

The first modern world exhibition is usually cited as the Great Exhibition of the Works of Industry of All Nations (London 1851, simply known as the Great Exhibition, or named after its main exhibition building the Crystal Palace). While there had been international trade fairs before the Crystal Palace, the scope, scale and design of the Great Exhibition really introduced a new form to world exhibitions. With thirty-four participating nations, six and half million visitors, and thirty-three million cubic feet of displays, the very scale of the exhibitions was remarkable (Greenhalgh 1988: 14). But it was the Crystal Palace itself which was innovative: 'the Crystal Palace was a gigantic structure of iron and glass dedicated to a new way of looking, that of the potential consumer' (Olalquiaga 1999: 31).

World exhibitions often cloaked their intentions in the rhetoric of moral and aesthetic improvement or in such slogans as 'peace through understanding', yet their commercial nature was never far from the surface. Visitors complained that the Crystal Palace was 'neither crystal nor a palace, it was a bazaar' (cited in Olalquiaga 1999: 32). The anthropologist Burton Benedict argued that the educational role of world exhibitions constantly had commercial ends:

> The goods shown at world's fairs did not just cater to middle-class taste, they helped form that taste. People were to be educated about what to buy, but more basically they were to be taught to want more things, better quality things and quite new things. At world's fairs this education took on society-wide and even international dimensions. The consumer society was being born.
>
> (Benedict 1983: 2)

In a different register this is also the claim made by Walter Benjamin when he described world exhibitions as places of pilgrimage. Such religious associations would not have been lost on Queen Victoria when she wrote in her diary of attending the Great Exhibition: 'One felt filled with devotion, more so than by any [religious] service I have ever heard' (cited in Olalquiaga 1999: 36).

Writing about the world exhibition of 1867 (set in Paris) Benjamin, claims that 'the phantasmagoria of capitalist culture attains its most radiant unfolding in the World Exhibition' (1999: 8). We should pay attention to the choice of words here: world exhibitions are the showcases of commodity culture (capitalism's insistent production) but they are a particular kind of showcase, one that requires concentrated light (natural or artificial). The use of light is a crucial aspect of the sensual transformation that the thing undertakes when it becomes a commodity and it is part of the sensual realm that we, as passionate consumers, respond to. For Benjamin the phantasmagoria isn't just a metaphor for the way that things become ghostly apparitions in consumer culture but refers to the actual magic lantern displays that featured the illusionistic conjuring of phantoms, which were exhibited in Europe at the end of the eighteenth century and the beginning of the nineteenth, under the name 'phantasmagoria'. Terry Castle's description of phantasmagoric displays shows how the educational intention of the display is a cover for something more affective, more passionate:

> The early magic-lantern shows developed as mock exercises in scientific demystification, complete with preliminary lectures on the fallacy of ghost-belief and the various cheats perpetrated by conjurers and necromancers over the centuries. But the pretense of pedagogy quickly gave way when the phantasmagoria itself began, for clever illusionists were careful never to reveal exactly how their own bizarre, sometimes frightening apparitions were produced. Everything was done, quite shamelessly, to intensify the supernatural effect. Plunged into darkness and assailed by unearthly sounds, spectators were subjected to an eerie, estranging, and ultimately baffling spectral parade.
>
> (Castle 1995: 143)

This intensification of effect and affect of passion is the result of creating a sensual environment that uses light (and, just as importantly, darkness) and sound.

World exhibitions, then, not only put objects on display they make them desirable through a process of sensual reordering. When Burton Benedict describes the way that world exhibitions mobilise a range of techniques to impress visitors, at least three of these can be read as techniques for sensual adjustment: abundance, gigantism, and miniaturisation (Benedict 1983: 15–18). Examples would include the following: a large-scale monument of a knight on a horse made entirely from prunes (abundance); a working typewriter that was fifteen foot high and weighed fourteen tons (gigantism); a display of an urban development that showed 'half a million individually designed houses, more than a million trees of eighteen species and fifty thousand automobiles of which ten thousand were in motion over highways and bridges' (miniaturisation, as well as abundance) (Benedict 1983: 17).

The effects and affects of such a sensual world can best be seen in E. L. Doctorow's novel *World's Fair*, which describes the 1939–1940 New York World's Fair. The novel comes to a narrative crescendo when the protagonist (a young boy) eventually visits the fair, determined to see all its wonders. The novel describes the colossal spectacle and the reaction of the boy as he careers from one pavilion to the next. Confronted by the insistent re-scaling of the world by the fair's displays, the boy moves from pavilions presenting the world in miniature (the General Motors pavilion and the Consolidated Edison exhibit) to those displaying gigantic versions of body parts (the Public Health Building). The effect is vertiginous: 'I was made light headed by the looming and shrinking size of things' (Doctorow 1985: 243). Similarly in Miles Beller's novel of the same world's fair, the experience of visiting the General Motors' pavilion (the one with half a million houses and million trees) is also described in a dizzying way: 'The future made you swoon, shaky in the knees. The future made you small and insignificant, nominal in the big picture' (Beller 2000: 17).

But it was the use of light as much as these distortions of scale that allowed world exhibitions to inspire the passions of awe and veneration. And importantly it was the use of light that allowed a number of seemingly immaterial phenomena to take material form, and to take their place as desirable commodities. For instance how would you make the delights of electricity vivid? The answer at the 1933–34 Century of Progress Exposition in Chicago was provided by the Electrical Building

> The lighting designers at the Century of Progress surpassed the Spanish fairs [the Barcelona and Seville expos of 1929] by using gaseous tube lighting for the first time at a world's fair. In most cases the tube lighting was seen only as a reflected light, but on the exterior wall of the Electrical Building, nearly a mile of green and blue tube lighting resembled a fifty-five-foot-high waterfall.
> (Rydell, Findling and Pelle 2000: 80).

At the 1964–5 New York World's Fair it was provided by the 'Tower of Light', a pavilion sponsored by a national consortium of electrical utility companies and was designed to transform the intangibility of light into a solid mass, a tower. The pavilion itself looked uncannily like the Emerald City in *The Wizard of Oz*, and emerging from this glowing crystalline assemblage was a beam of light produced by twelve one billion-candlepower searchlights (the equivalent of 340,000 car headlights). Light, as a commodity, became a solid object, a thing, produced from within the magical city and bearing magical properties.

The 1939–40 New York World's Fair provides a vivid demonstration of illuminating the city for the purpose of the commodity. The Consolidated Edison pavilion staged a display called the 'City of Light' which was at the time the world's largest diorama. Presenting a three dimensional relief of the Manhattan skyline, the designer Walter Dorwin Teague, offered an image of the city pulsed to the rhythm of electricity. Spectators watched as the city falls into darkness. And just as night is about to completely envelop the city, a flood of artificial brilliance coincides with a voice telling you 'this is the city of light, where night never comes... a world of power at the motion of a hand' (Harrison 1980: 52). Light here bears the attributes of the commodity; it becomes both thing-like and magical, a form that brings life to inert objects. The city is made into an animated environment only on condition that it gives itself up to light in its commodity form.

Services like electricity have to be made manifest to be desired. In the second half of the twentieth century the challenge became how to make manifest the properties and possibilities of two new forces in the world, nuclear energy and computers, and to do so in a way that would seduce the consumer. Awe and wonder was what was needed. I'm going to concentrate here on the way that computers were presented in 1964, and to treat this as an object lesson in the passionate production of consumer desire. In the New York World's Fair of 1964–5 IBM, who had been developing computer technology for some time, presented a pavilion that was designed by Kevin Roche (the building) and Ray and Charles Eames (the display). It consisted of a 'grove of man-made steel trees', a rusted forest of 32-foot-high, tree-shaped, supports that provided a canopy that housed a number of different exhibits. Arranged beneath the canopy were; small puppet theatres designed by Ray Eames and featuring Sherlock Holmes and Dr Watson; probability displays; and data processing systems. The main element of the pavilion was a gigantic ovoid structure consisting of a concrete shell overlaying a steel frame and mesh that was perched on top of the canopy's roof. The outer surface of the 'egg' was covered with the letters

Figure 4.1 IBM Pavilion at the New York World's Fair 1964–5, courtesy of Kevin Roche John Dinkeloo and Associates.

IBM repeated nearly 3,000 times. The ovoid dome was part of the Information Machine; a multi-media theatre which presented a film and slide-show called 'Think' designed by Charles and Ray Eames.

The educational idea of the pavilion, and of 'Think' in particular, was to demystify computers. To this end the content of the display was determinedly work-a-day and domestic. For instance, in offering examples of how closely aligned everyday life and computer operations are, 'Think' offered spectators an image of a male football coach working on team strategies. The computations of the possible moves he works on are similar (according to 'Think') to the computations performed by the IBM processor. Switching genders 'Think' suggested forms of computation (demeaningly) 'appropriate' to women's everyday life. IBM and Charles Eames pictured a woman busily working out a seating plan for a dinner party. The gendered address of this material is a recognisable aspect of its historical moment and is, I would guess, part of the project of making computers as 'normal' as possible. Everyday life, in its most normative form, is the insistent message of the display: football, weather, dinner parties and so on. Yet the everydayness of the display, while constantly stressed in the supporting catalogue, seems entirely absent from the experiential form that the display took.

The everydayness of the content is propped onto a display technique that conjures up the exact opposite of demystification: awe, wonder and fear. While this might not sit easily with the declared intention of IBM, Charles and Ray Eames had for some time been fashioning an approach to exhibiting that employed a pedagogic approach based as much in magic and the fairground as in reasoned explanation. Magic is the term used by Charles Eames to describe his relationship with science:

> I was raised in a nineteenth-century mode, where my first experience with science involved minor physics experiments done almost as parlor tricks, mathematics through magic squares and electricity by way of a 'shocking machine' which was reputed to have some therapeutic value. All this had an aura of magic about it.
> (Charles Eames cited in Kirkham 1995: 264)

Shocks, tricks and fantastic effects suggest that the Eameses could be seen as mobilising 'thingly passions' in their display.

Always attuned to the theological repercussions of modern commodity culture, Benjamin's sense of a sacred realm for the commodity gets echoed in contemporary description of the Information Machine. *Life*, for instance, suggested that: 'in this punctual *deus ex machina* the designers have hit a Dionysian button calling up emotions of awe, terror, recognition and joy that are far more religious than those which Michelangelo's *Pietà* evokes' (Scully 1964: 9). *Life* magazine's pronouncement of the display as akin to a religious performance is only apparent when the whole display event is taken into account. To experience the Information Machine you first took your seat (along with about 500 others) on the 'People Wall'. This was a 45-degree rack of seating that was positioned so that the occupants looked out at the World's Fair crowds, while at the same time those crowds could view the wall of people as a spectacle. Once everyone was seated the entire wall of people was hydraulically lifted some 53 feet into the belly of the Information Machine. This mass becomes a unit as it is hydraulically moved into the 'egg' of the information machine. In terms of machinic relations, and in terms of the specificity of computer technology, this unit becomes a unit of memory, to be written on by the computational machine. Indeed the uploading wall (of 500 'human-bites') uncannily predicts the drive units that were just about to revolutionise computer technology. To see this display technology simply in terms of visuality would miss the performativity of the Information Machine.

Prior to this, though, a dinner-suited compère descended from inside the egg to relay some introductory and 'everyday' information. Once you had ascended into the interior of the Machine you were left suspended above a pool of water, which would be at least 50 feet below (much more, of course, if you are near the top of the People Wall). The passions of fear and wonder were mixed to produce intoxicated experience. Suspended above the water, the spectators were confronted with fifteen irregularly sized screens, projected onto by seven 35mm film projectors and seven slide projectors. What followed was a barrage of visual information simultaneously spread across the various screens. Eight stereo speakers supplied the spectators with Glen Fleck's narrative commentary and Elmer Bernstein's musical score. Leaving aside what was pictured on the screens, the actuality of the display *mise-en-scène* presents a vertiginous spectacle, experienced by an audience suspended in mid-air. Virtuality is also an aspect of this that is emphatically foregrounded by what Beatrice Colomina describes as the experience of being 'enclosed by images' (Colomina 2001). What this 'culture machine' is producing so vividly is a virtual world, where the spectators are displaced from a here and now to an elsewhere and an elsewhen. This removal of the spectator from an earthly realm into another world is carried out so systematically that the IBM visitors are quite simply lifted out of the world. Virtuality here is not the performance of disembodying, rather it unsettles everyday embodied experience. The body becomes a more fragile, a more tentative component in the display environment. At the same time however such fragility is replaced, or at least countered, by the viewer's integration into the apparatus, which renders the spectator as an informational component within a larger machine.

The Eameses pavilion, and the display techniques used in the presentation of 'Think', employ passionate culture. They utilise apprehension, veneration, desire, and wonder to promote new technologies and new commodities that promise to be tame and ordinary. Like the materialising of electricity they perform a transubstantiation: here the abstract mechanisms of coding and decoding are transformed into the material circumstances by which the frail human being becomes a side-effect of the world of commodity culture. Passions are the glue that allows commodities to attach themselves to humans: the thrill of danger; the lure of the erotic; the wonder of new sensual realms.

ADVERTISING AND FETISHISM

If in world exhibitions things are presented in a favourable light (often literally), then in the everyday world these sensual adjustments are made in a number of sites, in advertising (on hoardings, on TV commercials, on internet pop-ups and dedicated websites) and in shops (in store displays, catalogues, and again on dedicated websites). The shop windows of expensive department stores often provide a cornucopia of luxurious items or a staged display of manikins dressed in the latest fashion. Such displays are designed to provide passionate thrills, to offer a sensual paradise of earthly goods. Often though we see shops in the process of displaying its stock, we see advertising hoardings half-finished; a collage between last month's advert and the one that is half up. It is hardly surprising that the (unfinished) world of the commodity has made such an enduring topic for surrealist inspired photographers who are enraptured by the strangeness of a headless manikin and the abrupt juxtapositions supplied by reflections in the window.

The world of advertising is on one level a very ordinary surrealism: here cows speak, pigs fly, children are adults and adults are babies, machines have human characteristics and come alive when everyone has left the factory, and where humans covet their thingly world. It is a world where the term 'fetish' resonates as a dynamic mutable force. To call a commodity a fetish is, I think, permission to see it as not simply masking the real conditions under which it was produced but to recognise the way it can fulfil multiple roles and overcome the paucity of its actuality. Why would anyone believe that a small vial of strong smelling liquid (perfume) could improve anything in your world if it didn't also act as a talisman, a fetish that attracts magical forces to you while protecting you from those that would harm you?

When in 1867 Karl Marx wrote about the peculiar characteristics of the commodity he titled his discussion 'The Fetishism of the Commodity and its Secret'. In this discussion he recognises the commodity as the magical transformation of the mere object:

> The form of wood, for instance, is altered if a table is made out of it. Nevertheless the table continues to be wood, an ordinary, sensuous thing. But as soon as it emerges as a commodity, it changes into a thing which transcends sensuousness. It not only stands with its feet on the ground, but, in relation to all other commodities, it stands on its head, and evolves out of its wooden brain grotesque ideas, far more wonderful than if it were to begin dancing of its own free will.
>
> (Marx 1976 [1867]: 164)

For me this is powerful writing that really gives a sense of the anthropomorphism that seems such a dominant aspect of advertising and of the commodity itself. But I also think that Marx gets something wrong about the commodity when he says it 'transcends sensuousness', from my point of view it would be better to think of this as a process of transforming sensuousness, sometimes to the point of transubstantiation (take this perfume, this is my body). Marx seems to suggest that when an object becomes a commodity it stops being a sensuous thing and instead becomes an ideational thing making irrational demands and improbable suggestions. While I wouldn't disagree with the spirit of this analysis it strikes me as in keeping with other aspects of Marx's writing (for instance his claim that language is sensuous consciousness) to see processes of commodification as an intensification and refashioning of sensuous and passionate properties. That is to say that commodification doesn't simply take place at the level of the idea but also at the level of sensuous materiality.

Of course when Marx was writing the possibilities of sensuous refashioning were limited by the technology at the advertiser's disposal. Most adverts were rhetorical claims made using words; if there were images they were simply there to provide more information about the product being advertised. The idea of film was barely conceived and photography was very much a tool for realists rather than fantasists. These days advertising media is often at the forefront of cutting-edge direction and one of the things that will go to make a good campaign is a memorable sensual world.

Take for example a series of TV commercials advertising T-Mobile in the UK. (T-Mobile is a global mobile phone service provider.) All of the adverts show the urban environment as endlessly accommodating to the needs and physical presence of the young people featured in the ads. At times the city is soft and pliable, or radically mobile (houses and buildings move or can be instantly folded away) or else the city's dangers can be known in advance and avoided. The advert for T-Mobile 'Flext' (a flexible allowance tariff that lets you know by weekly text-messages how much allowance you have left) begins with a young man (in beige short-sleeve shirt and grey casual trousers) talking on his cell-phone in a high-rise apartment. He walks out of the French doors on to the balcony and over the edge, where he falls onto the paving stones below. He is shown from above falling in slow-motion (and still talking nonchalantly on his phone); when he hits the ground, instead of this mangling his body, the entire ground cushions him, like a giant loose trampoline or a giant waterbed, and bounces him upright again. He gets a lift on the side of a delivery truck whose side panel softly moulds to fit him. He walks passed a café where he sees a friend; he

Figure 4.2   T-Mobile Flext advert, with kind permission T-Mobile and Rebecca Blond Associates.

reaches out to touch 'hello' to her and the windowpane responds to his touch like a thin plastic (and endlessly flexible) membrane. As he walks through a park the trees bend to give him consistent and endless shade.

The advert feels dreamy. The soundtrack to it (and a central component of the advert's feel) was a relatively obscure song from 1970 by the folk singer Vashti Bunyan (of course the success of the advert has made the song a big seller). The song is lilting, airy and harks back to the cadences of traditional English folk music; Vashti Bunyan sings in a breathy, ethereal voice. For T-Mobile the music that accompanies their adverts is crucial: 'We try to use new tracks by up and coming artists (we'd love our ad to take a musician's career to the next level). But more importantly, we try to pick songs that are especially whistleworthy, hummable, singable – or all of the above' (T-Mobile UK website). The ethereal voice accompanies a man moving through a city where normal physics is being reanimated and sensuously transformed: the concrete slabs wobble like jelly; toughened sheet glass bends to the touch, and so on. The hard and harsh material world becomes soft and pliable: it now bends to your will, your desire.

In another T-Mobile advert the images work to materialise their corporate mission:

> T-Mobile brings over 16 million people in the UK closer in touch with everything that's important to them. That means people such as family, friends and workmates, and the things that matter to them, like the football score, their favourite music and email.
> (T-Mobile UK website)

In an advert that 'makes the world flat for T-Mobile's friends', young people are seen talking to each other on mobile phones. As they move towards each other the impediments of the built environment simply fold away: gigantic office buildings collapse on themselves to allow the young people an uninterrupted journey to their destinations; tracts of suburban housing flattens itself to make way for mobile phone-wielding youth. Such adverts transform the sensual world and generate sensual and passionate desire for commodities. Here T-Mobile render a world of soft, endlessly accommodating sensuality for that most abstract of things: a tariff agreement.

In one sense there is no pure sensual aesthetic role for the commodity, no single hierarchy of taste. In an essential way commodity culture rings the death knell of a belief in aesthetic consistency: 'From Autumn to Spring the aesthetic changes. One talks of the eternal canons of beauty when two successive catalogues of the Bon Marché confound this drivel' (Jean Epstein 1921, cited in Marcus 2007: 2). Yet in another vein the commodity is aesthetic in the most literal sense (the Greek word *aisthesis* refers to the act of perceiving the sensual world). What lures us to commodity culture is both the sensual nature of the commodity and its performance of sensual transformation. And it is here where it can best be seen as an element of passionate culture – inspiring desire. But if the commodity lures us into its passionate embrace, passions are forms of attachment and dis-attachment, and in this sense commodities don't have a single passionate moment but become part of our passionate life. Between the shop window and the trash can lies the longer passionate life of things.

THE COMFORT OF THINGS

So what happens when we get these things home? What happens to the commodity after it has been bought, after it has lost the lustre of its newness, when it has been worn, used, consumed? Of course some commodities disappear, some fall apart, some things disappoint, but others will become part of your life. In the domestic interior is there really that much difference between certain commodities and the handmade gifts offered by children and lovers, or between consumer goods and the keepsakes we make for ourselves (photographs, for instance)? On one level of course there is (we enter into different relationships with the world of labour for one thing); but in terms of the way things exist within the home there may be less difference than we would assume.

The process that carries those commodities from the showroom window to take up residence in the home, sometimes adding to the homeliness of home, is the same process that fashions them as desirable commodities in the first place: sensual transformation. Yet while the sensual intensity of the commodity is often aimed at the visual register (the gleam and look of a new car, the cut and colour of a new coat) the homely thing is often characterised by a tactile sensuality. For Benjamin this was most keenly felt in the difference between a visitor (especially one with limited financial means) to a nineteenth century world exhibition and the amateur collector bringing bric-a-brac treasure into the home. World exhibitions, for Benjamin, 'were training schools in which the masses, barred from consuming, learned empathy with exchange value: "Look at everything; touch nothing"' (1999: 201). Here visuality is all, with the exhibition fostering literacy in commodity desires. At home with the collector, though, 'Possession and having are allied with the tactile, and stand in certain opposition to the optical. Collectors are beings with tactile instincts' (Benjamin 1999: 206). Of course we might need to adjust Benjamin's insights here; after all since at least the mid twentieth century 'the masses', perhaps especially those that can least afford it, have been encouraged to consume new commodities (both goods and services). Similarly the image of the collector needs to give way to the forms of everyday collecting that are much more informal than is suggested by the term collection; buying and keeping clothes, for instance, storing music and movies, and so on.

The tactility that Benjamin stresses is not simply the pleasure of touching certain materials (chiffons or plastics, for example), but of interacting on a habitual level with the world around us. When something becomes part of our everyday landscape it seldom draws attention to itself visually; more usually it takes up residence among us to be used by hands, walked over, bumped into, and sat on. Such tactility may well be a feature of a whole range of things whose primary function is to address us aurally or visually: I buy an MP3 player, take it home and start downloading my collection of CDs on to it. I will use it on train journeys, listening to radio podcasts or to favourite music tracks: I will create play lists especially designed to take me from Bristol to London to Brighton. It will, over months and years, become my intimate companion on weekly commutes. It will sit in my pocket or I will hold it scrolling down track lists, altering the volume, flicking through categories. I buy a table from Ikea, take it home, construct it, cover it with a tablecloth and then use it for years, eating at it, writing on it, reading on it, watching children do homework on it, feeling us grew older around it.

What is important, I think, is not to assume that the commodity world encourages visuality and the domestic realm tactility (such claims only work as far as they fit), but to attend to the sensual transformations of the material world as raw materials are fashioned into things which are mobilised as commodities and which become somebody's possession. So while a mobile phone and the network opportunities that come with it are paraded before me as a sensual world of soft spaces and luxurious and safe connections the actuality of my phone at home is both associated with this and an alteration of it: I buy a mobile phone (or get one with my tariff agreement) and immediately I want to change the ringtone, alter the look of the screensaver, add wallpaper to it. In the end I opt for my daughter's voice urging me to pick up the phone as my ringtone, and pictures of the kids for screensaver and wallpaper (I'm endlessly predictable). The advert selling the phone showed me pictures of friends on the screen: the trouble was they weren't my friends, my family, and while the city is no spongier than it was before, I do have that sense of touch when I get a text-message from home on a long journey.

In a recent book the anthropologist Daniel Miller picked a relatively random street in London and got to know about one hundred residents in the street. Picking thirty of them he wrote individual portraits of them and their relationship to the thingly world that they had drawn around them. Miller introduces his book in the following way:

> We live today in a world of ever more stuff – what sometimes seems like a deluge of goods and shopping. We tend to assume that this has two results: that we are more superficial, and that we are more materialistic, our relationships to things coming at the expense of our relationships to people. We make such assumptions, we speak in clichés, but we have rarely tried to put these assumptions to the test. By the time you finish this book [*The Comfort of Things*] you will have discovered that, in many ways, the opposite is true; that possessions often remain profound and usually the closer our relationships are with objects, the closer our relationships are with people.
>
> (Miller 2008: 1)

For Miller, objects and things are communicating vessels; they hold, mark and intensify the relations we have with the world around us, the relationship we have with ourselves, and most importantly our passionate relationships with those we love and those who love and have loved us.

Each portrait presents the reader with a sensual representation of the person's material world, yet while each individual's world is unique and while their relationship to the things that surround them is singular, what seems to be constant (apart from the case of a man who has absolutely nothing that seems to matter to him) is that forms of sociality are intensely and sensually articulated by the material things that they posses. One portrait is of Elia who lives in a world that Miller describes as 'magical realism': for Elia the dead are present in her rooms through the material things that have been theirs. Dancing is important to Elia and she has always taken pleasure in being a woman who wore beautiful, sensual clothes:

> Many of her clothes will never be worn again, but they give her wardrobe a double function as a kind of museum: the dress she bought when she was just eighteen; the furs; the black dress with scarlet flowers; the blue satin with its gold and silver brocade; above all, the fine Janet Reger underwear. These are lovingly stored away with other treasures of memory such as the bedcover that her great-grandmother made on her Greek island.
>
> (Miller 2008: 37)

Elia's possessions extend her, connecting her across time to previous Elias (the child, the teenager, and so on). They connect her to other places, to other people. They are part of the materiality of her attachments. Such objects are material embodiments of our passionate cultures, extensions of our passionate life.

As things circulate they enter a dynamic and passionate world, part of which they constitute. They sensually attract us, refashioning our desires and wants; but we too sensually shape the world that we possess. It is true then that the commodity is a possession in both senses of the world: it is a powerful fetish that possesses us, that makes us possessed conjuring up new feelings and desires, and yet we take possession of it too; we bend it to our needs and desires. In some ways the world of things is part of a larger world of sensual and passionate communication (Elia's grandmother's bedcover continues to passionately communicate with her). And just as things are sensually transformed by their social life (from factory, through promotion, to possession) the sensual passionate world is orchestrated by a whole range of machines purposefully designed so that we keep 'in touch'. And as the next chapter endeavours to show, communication media extends our passionate world in unprecedented ways.

5 Keeping in Touch

(On communication, media, and ghosts)

In this chapter I look at the way various communication media mobilise intense feelings. Most forms of technological reproduction (from the printing press to digital culture) have a history connected to magic, death and haunting: this isn't just an acknowledgement of the pre-modern history of communication but also a recognition of the media's role in passionate cultural life more generally. In this chapter we meet the early years of sound recording, we explore some imaginary photographs, and look at the way radio and television established themselves as more or less welcome ghosts in the home.

For the philosopher of communication Vilém Flusser human animals are peculiar not because they communicate (most animals do that) but because they store their communications: 'man is an animal that has discovered certain tricks for the purpose of storing acquired information' (Flusser 2002: 5). For Flusser there is a perversity in holding on to what is, in the larger animal kingdom, a necessarily fleeting phenomenon. Flusser sees the storage of communication as a protection against chaos, an attempt at stalling the ravages of time. The tricks that Flusser would have in mind would be all kinds of inscription and codes associated with writing, typing, binary code, photography, telegraphy, magnetic tape, phonography, radio and film. Our media systems store vast vats of information.

Communication is constantly stored, but it is also deleted, erased, discarded, and unless someone is tapping our phone networks, many messages are simply disappearing into the ether. We leave traces (as the CSI [Crime Scene Investigation] teams on TV constantly tell us) and these traces maybe banal or monumental. If we empty our pockets, look at our computer files, look around our rooms we see and hear traces both personal and public: here a photograph of a loved one; there a well-known song. People keep hold of letters, of pictures, of sounds and texts, not just because they are meaningful but because they are charged with passion. This CD is peppered with the feelings of the summer we first met; that picture was all that I have left of my grandfather; that film will always make me cry.

In a world of digital internet access, the media's traces of the past are just waiting for me 'out there'. I can listen to and see Martin Luther King give his famous 'I have a dream' speech in Washington D. C. in August 1963. I can see and hear the crowd cheer, recognise King's church-trained rhetorical skills, and feel their frisson of anger turned to generosity. I can walk into the National Portrait Gallery in London and see generations of faces staring out at me, with all their different needs and hopes and fears etched on their faces (or at least I think I can). Libraries and archives hold enormous reserves of information and expression: I can loose myself looking up the facts about various inventions; I can find myself again in the pages of a novel. But for all the mass of communicative material out there (and the internet is, I assume, for many the dominant means for both accessing this mass of material as well as for imagining it) we'd be fooling ourselves if we understood that communication was somehow easy, or efficient, or straightforward. Perhaps the internet will teach us not to want anything too specific, anything too particular. Go to it with vague ideas, or simple questions and it will take you to all its continual elsewheres; go to it with an imaginary website in mind, that would provide you with all sorts of connected material, and you will inevitably be disappointed. Perhaps an internet trained generation of the future will become happy with answers to questions it didn't quite ask, and the constant possibility of cash prizes designated for you alone.

Media history, perhaps more than any aspect of cultural history, is filled with strange convergences across time; accidental effects, and unforeseen consequences. Today we think of ourselves as networked or wired but this would hardly have been news to many people in the wealthy West at the end of the nineteenth century. Indeed it's hard to not think of heavy old-fashioned radios when computer companies are advertising 'wireless' devices as if this was the very epitome of futurism. The story of communication media, then, is hardly one that could be written as a simple narrative of progressive development: some technologies were invented for one thing but ended up used for another. For instance radio transmission was intended to aid the telegraph and the telephone system, with little ideas about the possibility of broadcasting to a mass audience (Briggs and Burke 2002: 152–63). Unforeseen outcomes and bizarre coincidences constantly feature in the cultural history of media. In North America, for instance, the telephone was advertised as a way of relieving rural and urban housewives' of their loneliness. But with the telephone all sorts of geographical rearrangements became possible; you didn't need to go shopping anymore but could order your groceries over the phone and get them delivered; factories and offices didn't need to be located in cities but could be connected to urban centres by telephone; consequently wealthier white collar workers could live in isolated suburban settings. This has led one telephone historian to comment that 'the telephone may have been implicated in creating the very conditions from which it was praised for having rescued women' (Rakow 1988: 209).

I can't offer a history of media here, that would be far outside the scope of this book, but we can look at a few moments of passionate media culture. For the communication historian John Durham Peters media history is also the history of ghost production: 'those who build new media to eliminate the spectral element between people only create more ample breeding ground for ghosts' (Peters 1999: 30). Or to recast this thought; those who dream of dissolving the distance between each of us produces new and strange ways of distancing us: 'communication as bridge always means an abyss is somewhere near' (Peters 1999: 16). It is the strangeness of media that I want to look at here, its strange ability to touch across time and space but to touch without bodies. The passions that media culture solicits follow the full palate of passion but here it is the chill of the uncanny that is the dominant mood.

LOST IN THE ARCHIVES

The Fallon photo library is a collection of over ten million photographs, stored in an eighteenth century country house on the outskirts of London. While the Fallon picture library seems to be reminiscent of other actual picture libraries (most specifically the London based Hulton Picture Collection, which has now been absorbed in the enormous picture agency Getty Images) it is in fact the fictitious subject of Stephen Poliakoff's 1999 television drama *Shooting the Past* (for the script see Poliakoff 1998). The house has been bought by a North American corporation (represented by the character Anderson) that intends to close the library and turn the house into 'the headquarters of the American School of Business for the Twenty-First Century – or the Twenty-First School for short' (14). It becomes clear that Anderson had been writing to the Library telling them of these developments, but that the letters had been ignored by the idiosyncratic Oswald (the archive's main cataloguer). Because the building work is behind schedule there is now no time to find a home for the mass of images (Victorian and Edwardian erotica, shop fronts through the ages, giant squids, and on, and on, and on) and all that the business school is interested in doing is selling the tiny fraction of financially valuable images and destroying the rest.

The picture librarians (Oswald and his manager Marilyn, Veronica and Spig) try to find ways of getting Anderson to change his mind, to try and save the archive. The library has no computer system that catalogues the images and at best this is done through a partial system of index cards: 'You think we have computers in here! – it'll take years to catalogue all this and get it on line... of course we have no computers, it's all in here. (*He taps his forehead*)' (Oswald in Poliakoff 1998: 26). Oswald is the mercurial archivist who knows the various byways and cul-de-sacs that the collection presents; without him it seems to be just a random collection of photographs. On Oswald's suggestion they try and use the chaos of the archive to out-fox Anderson, by squirreling-away the most valuable photographs (the Man Rays and Cartier-Bressons) throughout the archive; slotting them in amongst the hundreds of photographs of municipal buildings and town centres. But Marilyn's approach is more alluring: to try and get Anderson to see the value of this chaos by showing the possible stories that are threaded through it (and the implication by the end of the drama is that such an archive would, potentially, contain the threads of everyone's stories).

In a key scene Marilyn is trying to get Anderson to see the magic and the complexity of the archive. She has been allowed to tell only one story from the photographic archive, and she begins by presenting him with a set of images:

> MARILYN: It is important to watch closely –
> *She drops a picture of a child on to the table. A little girl of about seven, dressed in thirties clothes.*
> ANDERSON: A little girl?
> MARILYN: A little girl... yes.
> ANDERSON: Going for the heart strings then?
> MARILYN: I hope so.
> *She takes out more images of the girl, all portrait pictures of her.*
> MARILYN: A little Jewish girl. Lily Katzman. In Berlin –
> ANDERSON: Jewish too?... A Holocaust story? (*Softly.*) It won't be difficult to move me... I get affected very quickly by those stories... You've taken an easy route.
> MARILYN: Don't jump to conclusions.
>
> (Poliakoff 1998: 34)

We, along with Anderson, watch Lily, a German Jewish child living in Berlin in the 1930s, and move through the family photographs that her father, a keen amateur photographer, took of her. We learn that she was taken into an 'Aryan' German family for safety as the Nazis started their murderous pogrom of sending Jews (along with homosexuals, the disabled, and Romanies) to concentration camps. But because the library is such a vast archive Oswald has been able to find other traces of Lily in the background of other photographs as she picks her way across Berlin after a clandestine meeting with her father. She is there in the crowds of a parade, photographed by a journalist; she is there coming out of a bank photographed by secret police; and finally (it would seem) she is there being made to get on one of the infamous trains that would take her to Buchenwald or Auschwitz, to Dachau or Belsen.

These other photographs had been found by Oswald visually scanning the thousands of photographs in the archive of Berlin in the 1930s. When the library was given these images of Lily by her son-in-law (let's not forget that all these people and images are imaginary) the librarians were told that Lily had survived the death camps and had come to England and lived in the Elephant and Castle area of South London. Oswald, scouring the archives again, had found one last image of Lily: as a down-and-out, 'bag-lady', walking the streets of South London and appearing to shout and gesticulate aggressively at the street photographer taking her photograph.

In early 1980 the French critic Roland Barthes published what was to be his final book (a month after it came out he was hit by a laundry van and died a month later from his injuries). The book was called *Camera Lucida: Reflections on Photography*. It was a deeply personal book, written after his mother's death and with her very much in mind. Barthes writes about photographic images and how they affect him. In what is the central argument of the book Barthes suggests that the photograph has two aspects and he gives Latin names to them. The first is the photograph's *studium*. For Barthes the photograph's *studium* offers 'a kind of general interest, one that is even stirred sometimes, but in regard to them my emotion requires the rational intermediary of an ethical and political culture' (Barthes 1984 [1980]: 26). For Barthes the *studium* produces an '*average* affect', makes photographs seem merely interesting: 'it is by *studium* that I am interested in so many photographs, whether I receive them as political testimony or enjoy them as good historical scenes' (1984 [1980]: 26). This is hardly passionate culture for Barthes.

On the other hand Barthes suggests that the aspect of photographs that really moves him, break or puncture this *studium*. This is what Barthes calls the *punctum*. 'This element', writes Barthes, 'rises from the scene, shoots out of it like an arrow, and pierces me': 'A photograph's *punctum* is that accident which pricks me (but also bruises me, is poignant to me)' (Barthes 1984 [1980]: 26, 27). For Barthes it is the *punctum* that embroils our passions; without it the most that a photograph can hope for is a low intensity response. Barthes gives a mass of examples of finding the *punctum* within the generalising field of *studium* (in other words within the field of the sociological and culturally interesting): the strap on a pair of shoes, a bandaged finger: 'What I see [...] is the off-centre detail [...] the girl's finger bandage; I am a primitive, a child – or a maniac; I dismiss all knowledge, all culture, I refuse to inherit anything from another eye than my own' (51).

Barthes' book is a melancholic read, clearly written while grieving for his mother. It is also a book by an author who has turned in on himself, who is shutting out the outside world, while mourning in 'private'. You get a whiff of that mood in the words I've just quoted; a maniacal child or 'primitive' dismissing all knowledge, all culture. *Camera Lucida* is a great book for learning about Barthes; it has its limitations for thinking about photography as passionate culture. Primarily it fails to recognise the emotional intensity of the sociologically and culturally interesting, and this is because it only allows the interesting to be a sort of neutral emotional field. It also fails to see that the entire scene (not just an obscure element within it) can be a scene of passionate culture. When Anderson looks at the picture of Lily in amongst the crowds at a Nazi ceremony it is the juxtaposition of the small child amongst the pomp of Fascist ritual that is moving. When Anderson looks at Lily standing in a row with four other children waiting to board the train to God knows where, he mutters 'their little suitcases' (Poliakoff 1998: 40). But this isn't a *punctum* in Barthes sense: this is a detail of the *studium* that we recognise through cultural knowledge. The little suitcases are receptacles of possessions and clothes, of 'worldly-goods'. We have seen them before stacked up on the edges of platforms in any number of forced migrations. They are pitiful, containing remnants of dreams and hopes crushed by history. Unlike his other books where passions circulate intensely but also communally, Camera Lucida has, for a moment, lost site of the sociality of the passions, the way that they glue culture together. Here passion is what boils up from the singularity of a personal relationship (Barthes' with his mother). The social world is, for the grieving Barthes, just 'interesting'.

The word 'interesting' is an epithet that is often used to denigrate aspects of culture, to strip them of their passionate aspect. As Sianne Ngai has argued, the term 'interest' does emerge as a form of emotional detachment in the Romantic period, a sort of non-sensual aesthetic judgement, but as she also notes, in the psychology of William James it exists as the very basis for any form of passionate engagement with the world at all. For James:

> Millions of items of the outward order are present to my senses which never properly enter into my experience. Why? Because they have no *interest* for me. *My experience is what I agree to attend to.* Only those items I *notice* shape my mind – without selective interest, experience is utter chaos. Interest alone gives accent and emphasis, light and shade, background and foreground

> – intelligible perspective, in a word. It varies in every creature, but
> without it the consciousness of every creature would be a grey
> chaotic indiscriminateness, impossible for us to even conceive.
>
> (James cited in Ngai 2008: 785 italics in the original)

The *studium* of photographs interest us culturally, politically and
emotionally as passionate culture because we live in historical and
political worlds. To be interested in this visual field is not to give
up on the piquant passion of the *punctum* in favour of something
flat and dispassionate. Rather it is to engage in the visual world as
a passionate social being, to see the little suitcases as connected to
other little suitcases, to see Lily's story as related to other stories,
to see one image as part of an enormous archive and a succession
of archives that might be able to tell something of the story of each
of us.

Anderson and the librarians are looking at pictures of the dead.
Like the child in M. Night Shyamalan's *The Sixth Sense* (1999)
those who look at photographs see 'dead people, all the time'.
Photography as many theorists of photography claim, is a premo-
nition of death: pictures of you as a child record the death of your
childish self, and other photographs will inevitably record the decay
of your body as it heads towards what the novelist Raymond
Chandler called 'the big sleep'. But if photography seems implicitly
and unavoidably destined to record the dead, for many early practitioners this became a much more explicit activity. Professional
photographers in the early decades of photography specialised in
photographing corpses, mainly of older people who had died, but
also as a way of memorialising those that had hardly any life at all.
In Jay Ruby's book *Secure the Shadow: Death and Photography in
America*, the visual anthropologist explores the practices of mother's
posing with their newly dead babies, dressed in finery, looking as
if they are asleep on their mother's laps. Photography is always a
little death, but sometimes it is a big death too. We are touched by
photography (as one reaches out and tries to touch a shadow) partly
because an abyss has opened up between us and photography's
subject.

But if the photographic print can touch us through its visual sense
it was only one of a number of technologies emerging in the
nineteenth century that would alter our sensual world. In many
ways the sound and vision technologies of telephones, telegraphs,

phonographs, gramophones, film, televisions and radios would do more to alter the world of passionate, sensual culture than the photograph could achieve alone. If photography often seems to be obsessed with death, to the point where it has been seen to embalm the living, and to predict the sitter's death, then these other technologies are not just death obsessed, but insist on a range of other uncanny properties.

PLAY IT AGAIN

Many of us can't get through the day without our mobile phones (I must admit to not being one of those); some of us can't contemplate a train journey without being plugged into an mp3 player (I readily admit to being one of these). Telephones, phonographs and gramophones and their progeny – the mobile sound gadgets that seem to have become ubiquitous in the last dozen years for those that can access them – have re-orchestrated our sensual and passionate culture in perhaps surprising ways. For John Durham Peters:

> The succession from the 'singing wire' (telegraph), through the microphone, telephone, and phonograph to radio and allied technologies of sound marks perhaps the most radical of all sensory reorganizations in modernity. Except for echoes, hearing disembodied voices has, for most of the history of our species, been the preserve of poets and the mad. The phonograph was one of several sound technologies to democratize this experience, and as with most things democratic, the oracular edge has worn off with use. The phonograph presented a human voice without a human body. The human soul, the breath, had taken up residence in a machine.
> (Peters 1999: 160–1)

Peters is attuned to the strangeness that these new forms of communication embodied; voices without bodies, images without substance, a single voice in a million places. For Peters the history of media is linked to a longer history of communication that swerves between dreams of perfect one-to-one communication (for instance in telepathy) and solipsism (the idea that we are locked up in our own private worlds, unable to communicate much of it to anyone).

It seems clear from looking at the history of modern electronic media that they emanate from the dream of clear and perfect communication, but it also becomes evident that such media also increase the possibilities of miscommunication. What office environment hasn't erupted in a slew of bad-tempered emails in response to one that hadn't managed to convey the right tone (of irony, or lack of it) and consequently has managed to upset the entire office? Who hasn't received a text-message that was meant for someone else, some other Ben, or someone next in line in the sender's address book? Our communication machines are haunted by ghosts, and our culture is filled with images of this. Think of that young girl in the film *Poltergeist* who comes down for her bedroom at night summoned by the ghosts of the dead who live inside the television: she sits and stares at the TV static as the ghouls tempt her into their world.

Just as photography seem to be intractably connected to death (both in its phenomenal affects and in the practices of early photographers) so too does sound recording. In an advertisement for a gramophone from 1894 the machine is described as 'the only permanent means able to reproduce, in a *natural* quality, a living breath of air and speech – of those who will hereafter pass from this life' (cited in Sterne 2003: 305). For a while, at least, the sound recording industry was fascinated by the potential of the phonograph for what would have seemed like supernatural ends. One particular end was the use of sound technology for recording the funeral sermon for the recorder's own funeral (see Sterne 2003: 303–4). The famous painting used to promote the company *His Master's Voice* (now simply HMV) is of a mournful-looking dog (Nipper), with ears pricked, sadly staring down the inside of a gramophone horn. The suggestion that the dog's master is actually dead, and that this recording is the only 'animate' part of him left, is given more evidence when you look at the original painting. Not initially intended as an advertisement, Francis Barraud's painting was made not long after the painter's brother had died, and some historians have suggested that the dog is actually sitting alert on his coffin (Sterne 2003: 301–3).

The magazine *Scientific America* reported, in 1877, the invention of Thomas Edison's phonograph in the following way:

> It has been said that Science is never sensational; that it is intellectual and not emotional; but certainly nothing that can be conceived would be more likely to create the profoundest of

Figure 5.1 His Master's Voice – early advertisement for RCA Victor featuring their mascot Nipper the dog. Copyright: The Art Archives/Culver Pictures.

sensations, to arouse the liveliest of human emotions, than once more to hear the familiar voice of the dead. Yet Science now announces that it is possible, and can be done. That the voices of those who departed before the invention of the wonderful apparatus [...] are stilled forever is too obvious a truth; but whoever has spoken or whoever may speak into the mouthpiece of the phonograph, and whose words are recorded by it, has the assurance that his speech may be reproduced audibly in his own tones long after he himself has turned to dust. [...] Speech has become, as it were, immortal.
                (*Scientific America* 1877 cited in Sterne 2003: 297–8)

As Jonathan Sterne points out this was hardly stating a matter of fact: at the time of writing and for many years to come the method of 'capturing' the voice was relatively ephemeral; indented tinfoil, the initial medium, was absurdly fragile and would rarely survive its removal from the phonograph; wax cylinders, the next medium would not last too many repeated plays. *Scientific America* shows its over-eagerness; if only speech were immortal, if only we could live in the future as well as for the future. Sterne refers to this as the embalming of the voice, and of the phonograph as a resonant tomb, and by this he means that the voice is fundamentally trans-formed by the process of recording.

This sense that recorded sound produced a spirit voice vies and con-nects to the authenticity and authority of the voice in relation to the more distanced experience of reading. Recorded sound has the gravitas of those that speak from the grave, as well as the presumed presence of oral communication. The authority of oral presence was put to other ends by political parties who purposefully used the phenomenal affects of sound recording for propaganda purposes. In Germany, for instance, one important example:

> [...] was Goebbels's innovative and synergetic use of every avail-able medium, especially the development of sound/image propa-ganda, and his devaluation of the written word, because reading implied time for reflection and thought. In one election campaign in 1930, Goebbels mailed 50,000 phonograph records of one of his own speeches to specially targeted voters.
>
> (Crary 1997: 422)

Here the ghostly voice in the front room will become one of the murderous architects of Lily's desperate journeys in Berlin in the years to come.

By way of a coda to this section I should note that passionate cul-ture (even uncanny passionate culture) entails exuberance as much as melancholy, laughter as much as grief. On March 28 2008 BBC Radio in London reported that American sound researchers had found a recording that preceded Thomas Edison's recordings by seventeen years. The recording was 'made on April 9, 1860, by Parisian inventor Edouard-Leon Scott de Martinville on a device called the phonautograph that scratched sound waves onto a sheet of paper blackened by the smoke of an oil lamp' (Reuters online March 27, 2008). When the story was reported on the radio, the BBC played the sound recording of 'the first recording of a human voice, singing *Au Clair de la Lune*'. Following the song the announcer, Charlotte Green, broke down in a fit of barely sup-pressed giggles. As she described it; 'I'm afraid I just lost it, I was completely ambushed by the giggles' (*Guardian*.co.uk Friday 28 March 2008). It turned out that someone had whispered to her that it sounded like a 'bee buzzing in a bottle'; it did. Speech, or singing, it would seem, could be immortal, but at the cost of this voice being transmogrified, turned into the buzzing of a bee.

For Jonathan Sterne this transmogrification is akin to the embalming techniques used on corpses in the nineteenth century to hold back the ravages of time. Listening to that voice singing *Au Clair de la Lune* was something like looking at the dark shrunken and wrinkled heads that seem to inhabit most natural history museums I've been to. You know that this head was once human, but all that is left is a weatherbeaten charred doll: both funny and macabre. This is what immortality looks like and sounds like; no wonder Charlotte Green got the giggles. But if such an exuberant response fits the absurdity of the dreams of communication storage, it is the mood of the uncanny that we need to follow as these technologies take us much nearer to the present in the shape of television and radio broadcasting.

BROADCASTING THE UNCANNY

There is something at once ethereal and banal about radio and television. To have a box sitting in the privacy of your home telling you and showing you the latest atrocities occurring round the world, or playing you the current music sensation is, or could be, a disturbing phenomenon. From one perspective the history of broadcasting media has been a history of attempting to overcome the alienating affects of having disembodied voices and ghostly visions emanating from domestic furniture. How radio and television have become a domestic and sometimes comforting appliance has taken the skill and accident of generations of those involved in broadcasting production.

You can get a sense of how broadcast media has produced a feeling of friendly intimacy by watching old television interviews from the 1950s (available nowadays on the internet). In an interview on BBC television from 1957 a newscaster is interviewing a director of the nuclear energy industry. The occasion was the graphite fire at the Windscale Nuclear Reactor in Cumbria, England (it was renamed Sellafield in 1981): a catastrophic event in the history of nuclear energy and the industry is still dealing with the contaminated reactor. The TV interview makes for uncomfortable viewing, not just because of the enormity of the situation, but because the various protocols for TV interviews are not yet in place. The interviewee, who is claiming that there is nothing to worry about and that all safety measures were in place, doesn't know whether to look at the camera or the interviewer. In this constant shifting of eyes from one place to the other, he looks, literally, shifty. In our time when heads of state are routinely referred to by the first names, the interview seems to be stilted, anxious, overly formal and stiff. The 1950s interviewer doesn't engage the interviewee in conversation or argument, but asks questions and waits for answers. The 1957 interview has no flow, it is abrupt, starched.

Just how much broadcasting media is dedicated to the smooth flow of voices and images is brought home in the wake of more recent catastrophic events. For many people the mass killing of three thousand people in New York on September 11, 2001 happened 'live'. How can television function when all it can do (for reporters and viewers alike) is look on in horror? While the cameras impassively recorded the events, the news crews worked to conjure commentary out of devastation; the usual machinery of opinion-making ground to a halt, mesmerised by the terrible collapse of the skyline and the destruction of the human bodies it took with it. If TV regulates the flow of information (and smoothes it out) it crumbles in the face of events that supersede its information capacity (Western television had no such speech impediment recording and describing the *planned* devastation of Iraq that followed). The stuttering of television was also a characteristic of the morning news after Princess Diana died: the news got stuck, like a CD caught on an endless musical phrase, it was like watching nothing happening (it already had).

In the early days of radio and television the uncanny (in German the term uncanny is *unheimlich*, literally un-homely) characteristic of these media was much more explicit. For instance in Germany: 'Television in 1929 was regarded as the uncanny occurrence of the supernatural or marvellous in one's own living room' (Andriopoulos 2005: 620), and this emphasis on the supernatural was underscored by adverts for TVs including objects such as crystal balls within their advertising. The labour of broadcast media has been to make this uncanny state of affairs homely, to domesticate it. For John Durham Peters contemporary broadcast media, and he has in mind radio, presents us with: 'Intimate sound spaces, domestic genres, cozy speech styles, and radio personalities'

(Peters 1999: 215). Newscasters talk to us in relaxed convivial voices, sound recording privileges the rich lower registers and seem to talk to us in disarmingly intimate ways. Today it seems as if it is rare for radio DJs to broadcast alone. Instead they bring their chums with them and we listen in as if personally invited into an inner-circle to enjoy their jovial banter. In this there is no mass audience tuning into the ether; instead we are beckoned as individualised individuals, as unknown intimates.

Broadcasting media can be seen as a social technology addressing us (but in the singular) as familiars who share their concerns. For Paddy Scannell this has become the dominant feeling of media:

> What shows up for us, in the contents of newspapers and in radio and television schedules, are everyday matters. Everyday things matter for us in the ways that they show up every day on radio and television and in newspapers. It is this *every*day worldliness that is the common feature of all three: this ceaseless engagement with, this being caught up in, this being involved with, this attending to, this noticing, remarking, observing, commenting, blaming, ridiculing, laughing, worrying – it is all such and other concerns that mark out the everyday concernfulness of what we read and hear and see every day in newspapers and on radio and television. It is this that justifies the usage of *the media* as a common term for the press and broadcasting.
>
> (Scannell 1996: 177)

Scannell's argument is not that broadcast media really do care (some specific broadcasts probably do, some probably don't) but that everything is geared to make this seem to be the case. The media's concerns become our concerns because they (and by inference us, the attentive public) are concerned with a range of topics, worries, phenomena day in and day out. And one way of showing 'concern' is the extent that broadcasting and media more generally will go to hide the uncanny aspects of new media. In this the phenomenal and sensual world of media is geared, absolutely, to smooth and comforting dissemination (however troubling the news is). But this energy that is put into smoothing-out the media is in large part governed by the phenomenal alienation that is intrinsic to it.

Rather than thinking that broadcast conventions have finally eliminated the uncanny from media communication, finally tamed it, purging it of its supernatural character, it might be more useful to think of it as domesticating the uncanny, of rendering the super-natural as natural. In a vivid passage from Michel de Certeau's *The Practice of Everyday Life* he conveys this sense of an ordinary uncanny promoted by broadcast media: 'Captured by the radio [...] as soon as he [or she] awakens, the listener walks all day long through the forest of narratives from journalism, advertising, and television, narratives that still find time, as he [or she] is getting ready for bed, to slip a few final messages under the portals of sleep' (de Certeau 1984: 186). For de Certeau these stories organise us (in advance) and are filtered into our dream life. Perhaps dreaming is becoming more like watching television; certainly watching TV often feels like dreaming.

The transformation of broadcast media into the uncannily-familiar and the cosy-supernatural has worked to some extent to smooth-out the phenomenal strangeness of TV and radio. As an antidote we might well look to the work of the artist Susan Hiller. Hiller's work has constantly stressed the strangeness of electronic media-tion, relating it to earlier cultural practices (like sitting around fires and telling stories). Born in Florida in 1940, Hiller has been work-ing in Britain since 1967; she wasn't initially educated as an artist but as an anthropologist who became an artist partly as a way of renegotiating the Eurocentric and positivist tendencies within anthro-pology. In the various stagings of her video installation *Belshazzar's Feast* (1983–4) she uses video monitors to show a large, crackling fire constantly burning: in one version four video monitors create a cir-cle so that it looks like a media version of a camp fire; in another the video monitor is positioned in a domestic sitting room in the place of the fireplace or, actually, where a TV might be. The soundtrack con-sists of reported transmissions that occurred after the nightly TV shutdown (in the days before twenty four hour television, of course). In her writings about this installation she describes her intentions:

> Nowadays we watch television, fall asleep, and dream in front of the set as people used to by their firesides. In this video piece, I'm considering the TV set as a substitute for the ancient hearth and the TV screen as a potential vehicle of reverie replacing the flames. [...] My version quotes newspaper reports of 'ghost' images appearing on television, reports that invariably locate the source of such images outside the subjects who experience them. These projections thus become 'transmissions', messages that might appear on TV in our own living rooms. Like the language of the flames

('tongues of fire'), and the automatic scripts ('writing on the wall'), these incoherent insights at the margins of society and at the edge of consciousness stand as signs of what cannot be repressed or alienated, signs of that which is always already destroying the kingdom of law.

(Hiller 1986: unpaginated)

Hiller's point might be that the broadcast media's power resides not in its uncanny-ness but in the way that it sets up home in our most intimate environments as a convivial guest. To break the 'kingdom of law' might, for Hiller, include re-recognising its supernatural character, its uncanny aspects.

We use the term 'keeping in touch' as a stock phrase for asking ourselves and others to use various media for communicating across distance and time (telephone, letters, email and so on). We also use the term to talk about our ability to access information about local, national and global issues (to not know what is going on in the world is to be 'out of touch'). Yet this is for the most part an electronic 'touch', a metaphoric form of contact. If, to quote Peters one last time, 'communication as bridge always means an abyss is somewhere near' (Peters 1999: 16), then our use of telephones and the internet, or photography and television as a bridge

Figure 5.2 Susan Hiller, 'Belshazzar's Feast', 1983–84. Copyright, the artist; courtesy of Timothy Taylor Gallery, London.

between you and me, or between us and the forms of government and forms of centralised information and entertainment also suggest that the abyss is nearer than we think. Being in touch always means we have lost touch somewhere else. If artists like Hiller want us to remember this, it isn't to wallow in the grief of loss, but to temper our enthusiasm for communication, our happy willingness to play host to these ghostly guests. Keeping in touch might mean recognising this mediated world as spectral as much as spectacular.

6 Events of the Heart

(On love, sincerity, and hope)

In this chapter I want to explore a crucial aspect of studying passionate culture: how do you find the passions (so embodied, so experiential, so creaturely) in the 'cooled-down' world of cultural representation (primarily texts, objects, images)? In this chapter we look at the concept of experience as it is pressed into service for the work of reflection (description and creation). We meet the work of the philosophers J. L. Austin and Jacques Derrida as well as encountering the problems of sincerity, performance and realism.

The 'facts' of passionate culture are there for all of us from moment to moment: in the way your blood boils; in the way resentment gnaws away at your gut; in the cold steel of fear; in the lightness of exuberance; in the ego-less dispersion of some loves; and the anxious self-doubt of others. Perhaps for you resentment doesn't gnaw, but burns you up, or drowns you. We often frame our passions in conventional ways, but often too such conventions recognise the bodily truth of what might seem to be just a turn of phrase. To study the passionate culture of others (and so to understand the world in its connections and disconnections) we have to pay attention to these framings, and we also need to attend to the passions as they are often found in novels, plays, reminiscences, biography, letters, photographs and so on.

In the last chapter we noted that the idea of communication often vacillates between dreams of total, seamless communion (in the desire for telepathic communication, or of a pure unambiguous language) and the belief that the life of another is essentially unknowable as an experience (solipsism). Such a dichotomy is often played-out in other forms, for instance in the sort of absolute distinctions that some might connect to terms like 'objectivity' and 'subjectivity', or 'fiction' and 'fact'. If I raise a doubt about the possibility of pure objective truth in the practice of interpretation, do I necessarily open the flood-gates that will only allow in sub-jective conjecture? Or are there more negotiated paths to take that recognise the mediated nature of communication without having to immediately forfeit the possibilities of passionate culture being relayed through novels, films, diaries, photographs and such like, as well as through the cultural environments we inhabit and the daily exchanges we engage in?

It is the possibilities of such negotiations that this book has banked on. Passionate culture is a physical world of energies, of ups and downs, of high intensities and lower ones. And this physical world (and now more than ever before) consists of all the passionate rep-resentations that we meet constantly through reading, through electronic dissemination, and through our day-to-day minglings with the world. To siphon off 'representation' from the seemingly more concrete world of 'actuality' makes no sense when 'actuality' seems to be so stuffed full of representations. Yet to see pieces of cultural matter as simply transparent pathways to truth and exper-ience is naïve (it is the belief in the possibility of telepathy). Cul-tural matters are coded (often complexly, sometimes deviously): they require neither the faith of the literalist nor the cynicism of the radical textualist ('it is just representation'). What they do require is a politics of reading.

Communication might seem especially problematic when it comes to the passions. On the one hand there is, in everyday life, a whole set of problems to do with trust, sincerity and belief. If someone says 'I love you', they are quoting a phrase already used by billions of people before; how are you to know what precisely 'I love you' means in this instance? As the comedian George Burns used to say: 'The secret of acting is sincerity. If you can fake that, you've got it made'. So if interpersonal communication is fraught with difficulty ('are you really sorry?', 'when you say you love me do you mean the same things as when I say that I love you?' etc.), then the poss-ibilities of miscommunication, of fabrication, of play-acting might seem to be exacerbated when we read or hear about passion in more public culture. A politician being remorseful, say, or some-one pleading their innocence in a court of law, or a whole social group apologising to another group, are aspects of public culture where the sincerity of passion counts. How we might judge that sincerity, or whether, indeed, sincerity is the most productive prism for judging passionate culture is the theme that this chapter wants to open up.

Reading about feelings in another time and another place, lead to all sorts of complications: how do I judge the specific weight that a writer is giving to a word like 'pride'? Is Hume's pride, for instance, my pride? Or to put it another way: could Hume's pride recognise the sorts of pride being mobilised today in the name of cultural and identity politics ('I'm black and I'm proud', gay and lesbian pride marches, and so on)? Clearly a politics of reading passionate culture will have to do more than simply *want* to read in a certain way. It will require a keen sense of the historical valency and transformations of the passions, an car for their tone and timbre.

FACTS OF FEELINGS

Cultural studies, like other disciplinary fields, deals in evidence. The evidence it is interested in, what it takes as its objects of study, is often bewilderingly heterogeneous. It is not in the business of simply discounting certain materials because they don't seem to be reliable. Unreliable evidence (though this may seem to be a contradiction in terms) is often the best way to get a sense of passionate culture. In fact it would be hard to make a case for studying passionate culture only through the most rigorously reliable sources (when is fear ever simply true or false?). In 1939 when Britain was on the brink of war with Germany, Mass-Observation (an independent social research group) asked its team of voluntary informants to record their nightmares. Mass-Observation was interested to see if dreams could register the particularities of rising fear and anxiety (if indeed fear and anxiety were on the rise) as a country prepared for conflict. After the war began they also studied rumour: not as a way of discounting such material, but as a way of showing how beliefs and emotions circulated in culture. Such material is on the one hand clearly unreliable and fabricated; on the other hand it might also be the best indication of how passionate culture is being lived.

In 1937 Humphrey Jennings (a filmmaker, poet, painter and cultural historian, as well as one of the founders of Mass-Observation) began collecting the material for a project on the industrialisation of culture. The book, *Pandæmonium: the Coming of the Machine as Seen by Contemporary Observers*, was not published until 1985. Jennings worked on the book between 1937 and his death in 1950 (he fell from a cliff on the island of Poros, Greece, while location-scouting for a film). Jennings' daughter and his friend Charles Madge were responsible for the final shape of the manuscript and tried to fashion something that is as close as possible to the book that Jennings' envisaged. The material that Jennings had collected, and that Madge and Mary-Lou Jennings whittled into the volume that was published, is a collection of roughly a thousand pages of quotations with very little in the way of editorial commentary. For Jennings the book was designed to show how the industrial age generated a new passionate culture, how the machine got under our skin, wormed its way into our psyche.

For Jennings the rise of the machine constituted a major part of the material history of Britain. Pandæmonium is the name that Milton gives to the capital of hell in his *Paradise Lost* – it is a place of noise and disorder:

> The building of Pandæmonium is the real history of Britain for the last three hundred years. That history has never been written. The present writer has spent many years collecting materials for it. From this mass of material the present book is a selection. A fore-taste of the full story.
>
> (Jennings 1995: 5)

But this wasn't going to be a dry history of engineering and factory production. What Jennings was interested in was the feelings that industrialisation engendered; the new kinds of passions, emotional tones, fears, anxieties, perceptions, orientations that machine culture heralded.

In many ways *Pandæmonium* is a mass diary where the 'image' is privileged over the explanation. Images for Jennings are like fractals: 'I mean that they contain in little a whole world – they are the knots in a great net of tangled time and space – the moments at which the situation of humanity is clear – even if only for the flash time of the photographer or the lightning' (Jennings 1995: xxxv). The whole worlds that Jennings is collating are the experiences of machine culture as they are passionately registered in the recording of experience. They are passionate culture in all its wayward insistence. Jennings calls the materials he collages together 'events of the heart': 'They are the record of mental events. Events of the heart. They are facts (the historian's kind of facts) which have been passed through the feelings of the mind of an individual and have forced him to write' (Jennings 1995: xxxv).

Jennings probably puts too much emphasis here on the force of feelings to produce writing, after all nearly everyone included in the book is a professional writer of one sort or another (scientists, journalists, poets) and could be seen to have a learned dispensation towards writing. Jennings point about writing can be better understood, not as the outcome of experience (its translation, so to speak), but by asking what sort of writing would not be modulated by feelings, by the passions as they circulate within culture? If we can never really 'know' what it was like to experience a steam engine in the eighteenth century, or ascertain if a writer is giving an adequate description of it, we would be surprised indeed if a written account of an encounter with early industrialisation wasn't, to some degree, speckled with the passions of the time.

Experience is never simply the term we use to describe a singular event of one individual's encounter with something else: experience is such encounters as they occur *within* a passionate culture (or ethos), where some feelings are more available than others, where the currency of fear, pity and anger is already dynamically circulating in an emotional economy. This is, I think, what Jennings means when he writes about facts that have 'passed through the feelings of the mind'. Accounts of the coming of the machine, then, are not to read at face value, but are read as a way of delineating an emotional economy in which industrialisation was experienced, and which these texts contributed to. In practice this meant that Jennings' interest was as much attuned to the perceiving as to what was perceived, to the way experience was experienced (if this isn't a tautology).

Take, for example, this document from 1725 which describes the remains of a man who has been struck by lightening. It was published in the journal of the Royal Society (*Philosophical Transactions*, No. 390) by J. Wasse:

> The Shepherd lay partly upon his Side; the upper Part of his Head was terribly fractur'd, and his right knee was out of joint; He had a wound in the sole of his foot, towards the heel; his right Ear was cut off and beaten into his Skull, and blood flowed out of that Part upon the ground. All his Cloaths and Shirt were torn to small

> Pieces and hung about him; but from the Girdle downwards were carried away entirely, and scattered up and down the Field. Particularly, the Soles of a new strong Pair of Shoes were rent off. His Hat was driven to Pieces: I have a Hand-breadth of it full of irregular slits, and in some few Places cut as with a very sharp Pen-knife, and a little singed in the upper Part. His Beard and the Hair of his Head were for the most part close burnt off. The Iron Buckle of his belt was thrown 40 yards off, and a knife in the right Side Pocket of his Breeches.
>
> (Wasse cited in Jennings 1995: 36)

To start with this doesn't seem to be an experience of the machine at all, but an encounter with the effects of nature. It is also written in a consistently dispassionate manner. Now both these aspects are, for Jennings, there to be mined in an attempt to find 'events of the heart'.

This is one of the few entries in *Pandæmonium* that receives fairly extensive editorial commentary. Jennings situates this text within the context of the Royal Society and within a history of the colonisation of Britain by machines and the factory system (and here the Society's role seems to be the research and development department of bourgeois industrialisation). Before this though: 'an analysis of the materials and forces existing in nature and these islands' had to be undertaken:

> Among these forces was electricity – not merely as a source of power but also as an essential part of the development of chemistry. Electricity was studied among other ways by the study of thunder and lightning. Before these phenomena could be studied a radically new attitude had to be developed towards them, and to all natural phenomena. One of strict realism.
>
> (Jennings 1995: 37)

It is this 'realism' that allows us to see experience 'passed through the feelings of the mind'.

This realism (or any other realism for that matter) is not a transparent conveyor of actuality. What requires attention are all the ways of writing about this event that have not been chosen. There is no pity for the poor soul who has been killed, no remarks on the pathetic fragility of the human body in relation to the might of nature, no feelings of awe in relation to the mystery of God's will. We might call this dispassion, but perhaps we would do better to see this as a particular form of passion, a certain ruthlessness of curiosity that tries to expunge sentiment at every turn, a new utilitarianism that will be needed to herald the rise of the machine and be callous enough to ignore the broken bones that ensues:

> In this image then we have a contributor to the papers of the Royal Society giving a cold, inch-by-inch analysis and reportage of the effects of a thunderstorm equally without reference to God or man. Without a trace of human feeling for the victim or on the other hand of the ancient awe with which 'the glance of God' had been regarded for centuries, even ages, past.
>
> To do this required a new attitude. This new attitude is so clear and so marked as to constitute, I believe, a fundamental alteration of 'vision' parallel to that being developed by Defoe. Realism.
>
> Here then is a case of an alteration in vision already being achieved not merely as the *result* of changing means of production, but *also* making them possible.
>
> (Jennings 1995: 37–8)

Machine culture and the perception of machine culture inform one another producing new sensations and allowing such sensations to be perceived.

Pandæmonium is self-consciously concerned with the effects of machine culture, not simply on the lives of those experiencing it but on the imagination of those in contact with it. This is the story of the agency of machine culture, of industrialism not just as a human accomplishment but as an agent that transforms humanity and transforms the very way that experience is experienced. Thus the material that makes up the book is not 'factual' in any narrow sense of verifiable, it is imaginative – what cultural historians and anthropological historians might recognise as history from the inside, from the perspective of the native. The real is experience passed through the feelings of the mind, and those feelings are necessarily cultural, necessarily communal (though they will be very different feelings than those available to the shepherd out in the field). Such 'events of the heart' (and events of the heartless) need to be at the centre of the study of passionate culture.

PASSIONATE CLICHÉS

Baz Luhrmann's 2001 film *Moulin Rouge* is full of passion: it wears its heart on its sleeve (and then some). It tells the story of a penniless poet arriving in Paris in 1899. The poet, Christian (played by Ewan McGregor) finds lodging in the well-known bohemian district of Paris, Montmartre, where he falls in with a group of musicians, artists, actors and playwrights – the so-called 'children of the revolution'. Christian replaces a narcoleptic Argentinean, as the writer for the avant-garde show that the group want to perform (called, appropriately enough 'Spectacular! Spectacular!'). After taking inspiration from the absinthe they imbibe (the inspiration materialises in the form of a green fairy played by Kylie Minogue) they proceed to the libertine paradise that is the Moulin Rouge.

The Moulin Rouge is a cabaret, where men go to dance and to watch women dance, and where the modern is performed as a spectacle of sexuality, electric light, dance, music and alcohol. The main star of the Moulin Rouge is the courtesan Satine (Nicole Kidman). 'Spectacular! Spectacular!' has been commissioned by the impresario (Harold Zidler, played by Jim Broadbent) of the Moulin Rouge, and the bohemians want to convince him that Christian should write the show and that Satine should star in it. Meanwhile Zidler is trying to lure the Duke to bankroll the show by suggesting that he and Satine might become lovers. Satine (who is consumptive and will die of tuberculosis on the opening night of the show) thinks that sleeping with the Duke will allow her to become a proper actor, but mistakenly thinks that Christian is the Duke and so invites him up to her chambers and begins to fall in love with him (and he with her). The ensuing jealousies, mis-understandings, and the way this is woven into the plot of the show 'Spectacular! Spectacular!' is the narrative of the film. At the end Satine's dying wish is that Christian writes the story of their love (which is both where the film ends and where it begins).

But the intricacies of the plot don't concern me here. What I'm interested is in how the telling of the tale frames the passionate culture that is being so abundantly displayed on the screen. If this is passionate culture (and it would be hard to see it as anything else) then what kind of evidence is it of passion, what is it evidence for? The central characteristic of the film *Moulin Rouge* is that it works through quotation. And not simply any quotations; primarily it is anachronistic quotation. While you might find the occasional vapour trail of a jet aircraft trailing across the sky of a contem-porary film about the Roman Empire, in *Moulin Rouge* the vapour trails are insistent and they are consistently from the pop music culture of the 1970s and 80s and early 90s. When the main characters, 'the children of the revolution' (the name of a song by Marc Bolan and TRex from 1972), enter the Moulin Rouge, we find out that the dancers are called the 'diamond dogs' (the name of a song and an album by David Bowie from 1974). The music that they are dancing to is a medley of Labelle's 'Lady Marmalade' (from 1974) and Nirvana's 'Smells Like Teen Spirit' (from 1991).

These are not simply references but performed pieces of culture (both 'Diamond Dogs' and 'Children of the Revolution' are played in bits during the film). More crucially, though, during the initial encounters between Satine and Christian, and between Christian and the children of the revolution, the value of love is insisted on by reference to what might seem to be some of the most hackneyed bits of popular culture. Thus when Christian is being quizzed about his bohemian credentials he is asked if he believes in love, his reply is; 'Above all things I believe in love. Love is like oxygen. Love is a many splendid thing. Love lifts us up where we belong. All you need is love' (a mishmash of pop music titles, some from well-known movies).

When love begins to blossom between Christian and Satine, Christian starts to say how he feels: 'It's a little bit funny this feeling inside, I'm not one of those who can easily hide'. The line is from the Elton John and Bernie Taupin song 'Your Song'. Of course, Christian, like anyone else who might take refuge in the lyrics of a song at such a time, might, fairly be accused of insincerity, here especially given that the lyrics he is quoting seem to be contradicted by his actions (he is saying he can't easily hide, but is then appearing to 'hide' behind the sentiments of someone else's song). Christian starts singing the song with full orchestral accompaniment and what follows is an exuberant journey onto the roof tops of Paris as the song soars along with the nascent lovers: 'I hope you don't mind, I hope you don't mind, that I put down in words, how wonderful life is now that you're in the world'. How do we read this passionate material? Would the overuse of a phrase, for example, empty it of its passionate portent? Would its origin in the lowly realm of mass culture lessen its passionate impact: would quoting John Donne rather than Elton John seem to perform more passionate sincerity?

Moulin Rouge, I think, brings these questions to the fore, and suggests a way of exchanging an approach to culture that asks about the adequacy of a representation, to one that looks at how culture performs (and what it performs) and encourages us to ask questions about trust and doubt. In one way this takes us to a discussion in philosophy that began when the ordinary language philosopher, J. L. Austin, published his book *How to do Things with Words* in 1962. Austin's point, as he was the first to admit, was pretty simple, and he began by noticing that while language is often examined as a form of representation – as a statement of description – many uses of language need to be seen as actions that are only performed through language. Thus to say 'with this ring, I thee wed', or 'I bet you twenty dollars I can hold my breath for two minuets', is to perform an action through language rather than to describe something external to language.

Austin takes his insights further to make a claim that much of language is performative in as much as it acts on the world rather than tries to passively describe it. Even when we are describing the world, we might also be seen as attempting to convince someone else of the correctness of our description, and so on. For betting, marrying and all the other activities that language can do, to successfully take place (and Austin, here, isn't concerned about whether obligations like honouring the bet are fulfilled) certain conditions need to be avoided:

> a performative utterance will, for example, be *in a peculiar way* hollow or void if said by an actor on the stage, or if introduced in a poem or spoken in soliloquy. This applies in a similar manner to any and every utterance – a sea change in special circumstances. [...] All this we are excluding from consideration. Our performative utterances, felicitous or not, are to be understood as issued in ordinary circumstances.
>
> (Austin 1989 [1962]: 22)

Quotation, the sense of 'speaking lines' would, for Austin, hollow out the performative (and passionate) content of the utterance. It's a peculiar proviso to some degree since the examples that Austin gives of 'happy performatives' might be seen as scripted, either literally (the marriage ceremony has a script) or as analogy (we follow social scripts when betting, for instance). But we get his point too: two people getting married in a play won't perform the same action as two people marrying in a civil partnership ceremony.

Yet there is a tension here between the action of doing something in the world (convincing you, marrying you, betting you) and using the most worn out cultural items to do it with. It is also a tension between the guarantor (the sincerity of the performer) and what is guaranteed ('to have and to hold, in sickness and in health, for richer or for poorer I promise my love to you'). When the philosopher Jacques Derrida commented on Austin's book he argued that Austin's qualification of what counted as a 'happy performative' was false, since every statement is fundamentally either a quotation ('I bet') or could easily become one (he uses the example of a nonsense sentence – 'green is or' – being used as an example of nonsense sentences):

> Every sign, linguistic or non-linguistic, spoken or written (in the usual sense of this opposition), as a small or large unity, can be *cited*, put between quotation marks; thereby it can break with every given context, and engender infinitely new contexts [...]. This does not suppose that the mark is valid outside its context, but on the contrary that there are only contexts without any center of absolute anchoring.
>
> (Derrida 1971: 320)

What does this mean for passionate culture? What does it mean for *Moulin Rouge*? One way of reading this philosophical dispute might be to see Austin as alerting us to the performative hollowness of much of what takes place in cultural objects like novels, plays, films and so on. Derrida's position is harder to gage I think: is he extending Austin's qualification outwards and suggesting that all performatives are 'unhappy' (potentially); they are all hollow whether they are in a play or in a registry office? Or is he extending the performative power of language and wanting to see it as operative in both daily life and on stage and screen?

Derrida's position is designed to unsettle oppositions, and his unsettling of the difference between quotation and non-quotation opens up to unsettle oppositions like 'real life' versus representation (they are both saturated with one another). Yet we are still left in a predicament: is passion conveyed through these quotations? Are, to return to the film, Satine and Christian performing a passionate attachment or is this peculiarly 'hollow or void'? For

Derrida this unsettling of oppositions shifted the focus away from the text (what does 'I love you' mean) to contexts:

> One cannot do anything, least of all speak, without determining (in a manner that is not only theoretical, but practical and performative) a context. [...] Once this generality and this a priori structure have been recognized, the question can be raised, not whether a politics is implied (it always is), but which politics is implied in such a practice of contextualization.
>
> (Derrida 1988: 136)

Moulin Rouge establishes a context for its performances, one complexly woven across time: the now of the film (2001 or the date you watch it); the historical moment of bohemian Paris in 1900; the romantic pop culture of the 1970s and 80s and early 90s. Contexts are what connect us, what connects one element of culture to another. *Moulin Rouge* connects the bohemianism of the fin-de-siècle to the sentiments and sounds of songs and films that make up the cultural firmament of the late twentieth century (Baz Luhrmann would have been around twelve when many of these songs were at their peak of popularity). The bohemian belief in love has become a general element of pop music; while avant-garde fascination for the margins of life has become incorporated into mainstream culture.

But if *Moulin Rouge* contains such insights it does so not to judge (pop music isn't used for the purpose of parody, or to belittle sentiment) but to pose a further question: how can we love without trust? The question is also determinedly cultural. By circulating a barrage of pop music with such strong sentiments about love, about jealousy about those living on the margins, *Moulin Rouge* gives us an almost perfect example of what Jennings meant by 'the feelings of the mind'. What is crucial here is that we understand 'mind' not in the sense of individual consciousness or thought, but in terms of an older sense of mind as culture, as the social imagination of a time (the German word Geist has the dual meaning of mind and spirit, as in spirit-of-the-age). In *Moulin Rouge* the intricate weave of time and the possibilities of cultural quotation present us with passionate mind, emotional Geist for us to negotiate.

The challenge presented *Moulin Rouge* is whether we are going to trust this passionate culture or not: 'Without trust there can be no love', as one of the characters has it. Similarly the declared message of the film is: 'The greatest thing you'll ever learn is just to love and be loved in return'. But do we trust such sentiments; and if we don't trust them what are we left with? Yet it is a decision that the film poses without resolving. Do you trust the film, or do you treat it as a clever parody, surfing the froth of popular culture. If I choose to trust it, it is partly because it presents popular culture (many of the songs were hits when I was eleven and twelve) as 'mind', as the passionate culture which shapes our sentiments and sensibilities.

A politics of reading (though this politics might be multiple) has to deal with passion at every turn. Trust and distrust is threaded through passionate culture adding to the fragility of felt culture. But if love can sometimes be seen as a bohemian value that has filtered into popular culture, it also exists as a physical force, as the name we give to the strongest attachments we can find in culture.

LOVE IN THE TIME OF DESPAIR

In the Aboriginal Cultural Centre (*Bunjilaka*) at the Melbourne Museum there is a display called 'Koori Voices'. The room is dimly lit and the display consists of mainly black and white photographs of the Koori people and the lives they led and live in what became the state of Victoria, in Australia. The exhibition stretches from 1834 (the year when land-hungry and money-driven British settled in Port Philip Bay) to the present day. It is a display of oral histories and most of the photographs are accompanied by a sound recording that you activate by pressing a button (there are also transcriptions of the recordings by the images). A proportion of the exhibition is given over to the testimonies of those that make up the Stolen Generations. The smallness of the images, the darkness of the room, the quietness of the recordings produce an eerie intimacy: I don't know any of these people but I have to move in close to hear them, to see them.

The images are unspectacular: single portraits, or gatherings, or documents of activities. The testimony is invariably a straightforward accounting of facts, unembellished by rhetorical flourishes. But as you move in close, peer into the images, what you hear is heartbreaking. I can't remember too many details. I remember looking at a photograph of a middle-aged woman, and then hearing her voice as she spoke about the day she was out shopping with her two children. She went into a shop leaving the children to play outside. A few minutes later she came out of the shop to find that her children had disappeared. It was decades before she saw them again. Some parents never did see their children again; some children forgot that they had a mother. The children were taken – not by some serial abductor – but by the police, by the state.

I looked at a few more images, listened to some more testimony, but it became increasingly hard to see and hear. I was crying too much to be able to see properly and my body was starting to shake. The intimacy and the horror were too much to bear: I kept thinking of how I would bear it if my children were taken from me. Some didn't bear it. Amongst Aboriginal people one practice of mourning or expressing pain is to beat your head with a stone. Some parents, grandparents and siblings died from these 'self-inflicted' wounds. I was caught up in the blended colours of mixed emotions. Simultaneously I felt the fear of what loss could do to me; I experienced that fragility you feel when a new unknown dimension of suffering is encountered; I felt a mortifying shame in my national association with such a brutalising policy (as a British subject I was implicated by the British commonwealth policies of forced separations in Australia); and I felt a degree of self-disgust (as I do now) in thinking about my own feelings in the face of so much suffering of so many others.

The forced removal of Aboriginal children (and particularly of children of mixed heritage) was practised in Australia from the 1860s through to the 1970s (though this varied from state to state). The supposed legality of it rested on the colonial legislation that made Aborigines effective wards of the state. Children were removed from Aboriginal communities taken to mission schools where they were fostered to white families as domestic servants and farm labourers. Sexual abuse was common. Parents trying to find out what had happened to their children were lied to or simply denied access. The enormity of this policy was made clear when the Human Rights and Equal Opportunity Commission was asked by the Attorney-General of Australia to report on the history of these practices and the effects they had on Aboriginals and Torres Strait Islanders. Establishing an exact record proved impossible but the report concluded that:

> Nationally we can conclude with confidence that between one in three and one in ten Indigenous children were forcibly removed from their families and communities in the period approximately 1910 until 1970. [...] In that time not one Indigenous family has escaped the effects of forcible removal (confirmed by representatives of the Queensland and WA Governments in evidence to the Inquiry). Most families have been affected, in one or more generations, by the forcible removal of one or more children.
> (Human Rights and Equal Opportunity Commission 1997: unpaginated)

The report gathered together testimony from the children who had been removed, from the parents whose children had been taken and from various health professionals and social workers. The effects of coerced removal were felt (and continue to be felt) long after the events had taken place with many incidences of alcoholism and drug addiction and long-term depression being just some of its consequences.

On February 13, 2008 Australian Prime Minister Kevin Rudd proposed an Apology to Australia's Indigenous Peoples; it was passed by both houses of parliament of Australia. The apology included the following statement:

> We apologise for the laws and policies of successive Parliaments and governments that have inflicted profound grief, suffering and loss on these our fellow Australians.
> We apologise especially for the removal of Aboriginal and Torres Strait Islander children from their families, their communities and their country.
> For the pain, suffering and hurt of these Stolen Generations, their descendants and for their families left behind, we say sorry.
> To the mothers and the fathers, the brothers and the sisters, for the breaking up of families and communities, we say sorry.
> And for the indignity and degradation thus inflicted on a proud people and a proud culture, we say sorry.
> (http://www.pm.gov.au/media/Speech/2008/speech_0073.cfm)

The politics of passionate culture here is aimed at sorrowful remorse, at shameful regret. It also implicitly asks forgiveness: but that is not a necessary condition of remorse. You apologise by recognising past violence, not by wanting the slate wiped clean.

What are the 'happy' conditions that would allow this statement to perform, to enact an apology? What would allow me (or much more importantly the indigenous communities) to 'believe' the sentiment of this statement, to feel its passionate intent? A politics of reading wouldn't be able to judge in advance whether doubt or belief were the appropriate responses. It would be naïve to accept any and every apology as being sincere. But a politics of passionate reading means taking sides with what might be described as a 'guarded openness'. To want to believe the sincerity of a passion (here remorse) doesn't mean forgetting the past: if anything it puts the burden of the past into the present. If belief is to perform anything (Rudd's belief or anyone else's) its performance is a beginning rather than an ending. Walter Benjamin noted the follow saying: 'It is not what a man [or woman] is convinced of that matters, but what his [or her] convictions make of him [or her]' (Lichtenberg cited in Benjamin 1934: 98) and we might want to claim such a statement as a necessary condition of passionate culture. Guarded openness responds to the sentiments of an apology and watches to see what happens, what follows.

In 2002 the film *Rabbit-Proof Fence* was released. It was based on the book *Follow the Rabbit-Proof Fence* by Doris Pilkington-Garimara (her aboriginal name is Nugi Garimara). It tells the story of the author's mother (Molly) her aunt (Daisy, Molly's sister) and Molly's cousin Gracie. Molly, Daisy and Gracie were forcibly removed from Jigalong, an Aboriginal community in the deserts of Western Australia, and taken to the Moore River Native settlement, near Perth. The book and the film enact experiences that can be found in the *Bringing them Home* report: 'I remember all we children being herded up, like a mob of cattle, and feeling the humiliation of being graded by the colour of our skins for the government records' (confidential submission 332). Molly, Daisy and Gracie are similarly herded up and inspected to see if they are light-skinned enough to be fostered. The majority of the film (unlike the book) concerns itself with their escape and the amazing journey they took walking 1,500 miles back home to Jigalong along a rabbit-proof fence.

The film ends with Molly and Daisy returning to Jigalong (Gracie had been captured) and being reunited with their mother and grandmother. All of the story had been set in the past in the 1930s. The film (and the book) ends with an epilogue: in the film we see Molly Kelly and Daisy Kadibil now as elderly women in Jigalong. We find out that after Molly had returned to Jigalong she had got married and had two daughters, but that once again she and her daughters were forcibly removed, taken back to the Moore River Native Settlement. For a second time Molly managed to escape:

> Molly absconded on 1 January 1941, taking her eighteen-month-old Annabelle with her and leaving Doris behind at the settlement. She and her baby daughter arrived safely at Jigalong months later, following the same route she had taken nine years earlier. [...] Three years later Annabelle was removed and sent south to the Sister Kate's Children's Home in Queens Park. Molly hasn't seen her since.

I want the image of Molly as an elderly woman in Jigalong to burn onto my retina. A passionate politics dedicated to hope needs such images, needs them to orient its politics of reading (of believing and trusting). Such images are needed not just as a reminder of the brutality that can be meted out in the name of civilisation, but as a figure of hope, of an indomitable courage, of what is possible in the name of love.

7 Beginnings (in Place of an Ending)

This book has been designed as an introduction to the study of culture. It is meant to whet the appetite rather than fill you up. In this final short chapter I want to pose a number of questions for opening-up and pursuing the practice of studying culture, passionately.

In a book that is intended to stir a passion for the study of culture (not just enthusiasm, but mixtures of trepidation, wonder, anger, and so on) and to open up a space for the study of passionate culture, it is appropriate to end with a beginning. In this short chapter I want to briefly show how the way that a study of culture begins, fashions how it continues. Anyone who has tried to write a story knows how the first couple of lines seems to direct the rest of the narrative (its plot and its telling) so much so that to try and alter it substantially will often mean that you feel the need to start again. Yet the question of 'how to begin', of 'where to begin from' and of 'what to begin with', are not a set of questions that require absolute answers. They are, though, political and ethical questions. One way of tackling the questions of how and where to begin is to think in terms of productivity: what will starting out from here (rather than there) accomplish? What kinds of stories would it allow you tell and what stories would it exclude?

In Edward Said's *Beginnings: Intention and Method*, Said works to divorce the idea of a beginning from the notion of an origin. For Said 'a beginning is already a project under way' (Said 1985 [1975]: 13). This is useful reminder that a beginning is in many senses a meeting place, a nexus or nucleus of a constellation already gathering. To begin is already to be in the thick of things. We might say that we want to start with the concrete particularity of an object, a practice, a subjective experience. But haven't we already begun with a whole host of more abstract categories that have allowed us to recognise something as experience, practice and object? And haven't we some idea that this object, this practice, this experience is significant because it relates to other phenomena, other histories? To start with the concrete entails abstractions, just as starting out with abstractions entails the material, empirical world. A beginning is necessarily messy, necessarily incomplete: one complex place in a journey amongst many others. This should come as some relief: there is no perfect place to begin. But relief might also give way to responsibility: why start here rather than there? Beginnings might then seem to multiply exponentially: we should start everywhere. So as a way of helping to pick a path through this forest of possibilities, to find messy but productive beginnings I am going to pose a number of possible beginnings below: beginnings of historical periodisation and beginnings of disciplinary approach. But, be warned, this will just be the start of your troubles.

HISTORICAL TELLING

The activity of historical enquiry has been a constant preoccupation in this book. It needs to be central to any inquiry into culture. How else are we to recognise our contemporary moment as particular if we can't also recognise some of the continuities and discontinuities it draws on and leaves behind from the past? Historical telling suggests that we have in mind a particular duration, a significant temporality. Often this goes by the name of the modern (which, of course, is implied even when people want to address themselves to the pre-modern, or when, though this seems less and less likely today, they address themselves to the post-modern): it is a way of putting the contemporary world and its recent past into perspective. But the question of when and where the modern begins is not only contested, but entails making decisions about the way we characterise the contemporary world, what we take as the significant features of the modern, and whose experiences are going to be central or marginal to its telling.

Do we, for instance, start the modern in the mid-nineteenth century, in Western cities with rising populations of new migrants from the countryside and from other countries, with new industries rising up on its outskirts, and new consumer opportunities at its centre? You can tell productive stories from here, stories of the changing shape of cities, of the new experiences of metropolitan culture, of the spectacle of modernity emerging in new shops and the burgeoning entertainment industries. And of course it wouldn't just be a story of the wealthy fashioning urban culture to their taste. Anxieties and disappointment would feature heavily too as you watch the new petite bourgeoisie grapple with a field of cultural taste that seems to invite them and exclude them simultaneously, or as you see the new migrants attune themselves to the pleasure and pain that the city has to offer, or as you watch established trades fall into decline, and craft-based enclaves fall under the wrecking ball.

But perhaps we should start later: in the early twentieth century with the new factory systems of assembly line production; when advertising and design seem to begin to dominate production; when the international project to campaign for women's suffrage took hold and generally won. Or perhaps we should start earlier: in the eighteenth century and early nineteenth century with the Highland Clearances in Scotland; when the civilising mission of instilling manners and etiquette was at its height; when nation building was galvanising culture. It is almost immediately evident that to begin a historical period at a certain point also means locating it somewhere: in the US (for the assembly line) or in Paris or London (for nineteenth-century urbanism). Or to shift the focus from place to places; to begin with women's suffrage would offer us multiple perspectives, across nations, and thereby to start from a geographically more ambitious situation.

A single year is often a difficult time frame to begin history (it is more usual to think in terms of epochs), but some years appear in retrospect to be so monumental that they have some claim to inaugurating not just historical periods, but our sense of history itself. For Tzvetan Todorov 1492 was such a year:

> The history of the globe is of course made up of conquests and defeats, of colonization and discoveries by others; but [...] it is in fact the conquest of America that heralds and establishes our present identity; even if every date that permits us to separate any two periods is arbitrary, none is more suitable, in order to mark the beginning of the modern era, than the year 1492, the year Columbus crosses the Atlantic Ocean.
>
> (Todorov 1999 [1982]: 5)

We could link Todorov's claim to the work of Paul Gilroy and his project (discussed in Chapter 3) of understanding the Atlantic as a complex unit of multiple crossings and multiple perspectives: it allows history to be told from a number of positions simultaneously; from the perspective of being conquered and invaded and from the perspective of conquering and discovery.

Yet 1492 wouldn't just work to establish the Americas, their colonisers, and their colonised as the only agents within world-shaping history. John Docker's book is called *1492: The Poetics of Diaspora* (2001) and significantly shifts the focus from the Americas to Spain (which might not, in the end, be as far as it looks). 1492 for Docker is the year that the Jews were expelled from Spain and when Moorish Spain was defeated in Granada. Docker's book is one that begins with the end of something: with the ending of a symbiotic culture of Judaic and Islamic integration, an age of shared Indian, Arabic and Jewish culture. In our contemporary age of seemingly intractable Israeli and Palestinian conflict such a lost age stands out starkly as a historical cornerstone. 1492 heralds a new era of diasporic cultures, of cultural displacements, of homelessness as a general cultural condition.

But if 1492 might appear to be a year that many scholars can agree on, other writers have focused on specific years, not to argue for their singularity, but as a way of exploring the more ordinary contingencies of history and the cross-cultural networks that history generates. To pick a year, any year, out of a hat, so to speak, might be one way of getting more of a sense of the 'in-the-midst-of-things' of culture. Hans Ulrich Gumbrecht, for instance, in his book *In 1926: Living at the Edge of Time,* has produced what he sees as 'an essay on historical simultaneity' (Gumbrecht 1997: xiv). By taking a fairly random year (though it soon turns out that no year is random) he tracks back and forth across Berlin, Buenos Aires, New York and Rome, making connections and disconnections between these different contexts. Significantly his writing feels more like a small encyclopaedia (or a compendium for the largest cultural encyclopaedia possible) than an argument-driven, or narrative-driven history. He breaks up his volume into 'arrays' (Ocean Liners, Movie Palaces, Elevators, Strikes, Telephones, and the like), 'codes' (authenticity versus artificiality, center versus periphery, male versus female, and so on), and 'codes collapsed' (where the antagonisms of the codes get replaced by a new schema – life, tragedy, eternity, etc.). Each section of the book presents the headings in an alphabetical order, further emphasising the de-hierarchical practices involved. It is a heuristic book that places as much weight on the reader to connect and make sense of this cultural history, as it does on the author to produce a summation of 1926.

Marc Manganaro is more motivated in choosing the year 1922 as the title of his book makes clear: *Culture, 1922: The Emergence of a Concept*. Manganaro works around the year 1922 and works across literature and the social sciences to show how the very term 'culture' coalesces in around 1922 as a particularly dense and problematic term. For Manganaro: 'Nineteen twenty-two saw the publication of *The Waste Land* and *Ulysses*, as well as *Argonauts of the Western Pacific* and A. R. Radcliffe-Brown's first monograph, *The Andaman Islanders*, all of which effectively remapped the discourse of their fields' (Manganaro 2002: 8). It was also the year when W. H. R. Rivers died. To mark a beginning, then, always implies an ending, even when Manganaro is keen to assert that the history of the term culture is a process of threading various processes together. Michael North's *Reading 1922: A Return to the Scene of the Modern* also includes the canonical work of T. S. Eliot and James Joyce but also stretches out of this tight literary enclave to explore the way that the modern is figured in a host of other less literary texts (such as the work of Charlie Chaplin and Ludwig Wittgenstein, as well as a clutch of now-forgotten writers). To focus on a specific year because it is seen as a landmark year for the production of canonical culture can work to both reinforce this canon, as well as to displace the focus of the study of culture from a fixation on canonical and disciplinary specific texts.

In a recent collection of feminist cultural history called *Women's Experience of Modernity 1875–1945*, the spread of years is somewhat conventional (this would be a classic loose periodisation of what in painting, music, literature, and so on, would be the years of high modernist culture), but by focusing on women's experience it immediately alters our sense of these years. Ann Ardis, one of the editors, enthusiastically cites the writing of Rita Felski for re-orienting the study of the modern: 'How would our understanding of modernity' [be changed] 'if instead of taking male experience as paradigmatic, we were to look instead at texts written primarily by women? And what if feminine phenomena, often seen as having a secondary or marginal status, were given a central importance in the analysis of the culture of modernity?' (Felski cited in Ardis and Lewis 2003: 1). Our choice of years or year, our choice of duration and temporality also requires a choice of subjects, of agents, to fill those years with, perspectives from which to see history, to register experience. Like the 'slaves' points of view' the perspective of feminism allows women to take centre stage in a way that fundamentally re-orchestrates our understanding of the modern – not by sweeping over the traces of paternalism and patriarchy but by bringing them to the fore. Feminist cultural history works to show both women and men as passionate and gendered.

If there is no necessary 'right' time (or necessarily 'right' perspective) for the history of passionate culture, then there is, as I have been suggesting, an ethical and political (with a large P or a small p depending on you calling) obligation to describe and defend the productivity of privileging this time, this specific periodisation. But if the time is never quite right, are there are a set of analytic practices, or specific kinds of cultural objects, that would lead us most quickly into the midst of passionate culture? For certain disciplines the choice of analytic practice and choice of particular objects would, to a large extent, define their disciplinarity (what would art history be like if it didn't look at art works?). But what happens when a field of inquiry begins with the desire to work across and against the disciplines?

INTERDISCIPLINARITY AND THE PASSIONATE AMATEUR

Cultural Studies (as it was fashioned in Britain in the 1960s) was born on the fault-line separating art from science; a line (albeit a blurred one) that has come to separate the social sciences from the humanities. As such, cultural studies was, from the get go, formed with an interdisciplinary desire (or at least a cross-disciplinary one). Crucially, then, the desire for interdisciplinarity can partly be seen as a symptom of the disciplines themselves as they seem to harden into solid containers with an inside and an outside. This hardening can occur when areas of study internalise a set of protocols and techniques that become the pass-key for entry into their hallowed interiors. In the 1960s many of the disciplines that exist today went through a moment of extensive professionalisation that included adopting certain technical and theoretical devices, specialised terminology and canonical texts. For some the more technologically seeming the better. And of course Cultural Studies was not immune to these theoretical passions or technophilic tendencies; indeed in many ways it led the way. Thus Cultural Studies was both the desire for interdisciplinarity as well as incorporating the very tendencies that characterised disciplinary hardening in the first place.

The danger of setting up a discipline or a specialism as an inter-discipline or cross-discipline is that it immediately obscures the interdisciplinary work happening within and across the disciplines (in those arenas where the disciplines are not so hardened). If one arena declares itself as *the* site for interdisciplinary work, why look elsewhere for it? The more permanent damage, though, is it produces a sort of cultural amnesia where people forget what the study of culture looked like before the disciplines hardened into defended spaces in the first place. While there might not have been a subject area called 'cultural studies' in the 1930s or the 1890s there is a good deal of work in these and other decades that deserves to be seen as crucial examples of a spirit of descriptive questioning that should be at the heart of an enterprise like Cultural Studies.

In the contemporary academic firmament the desire of Cultural Studies can be seen to have dispersed. Academic disciplines routinely stray across boundaries, scouting for interesting ways of operating from neighbouring and distant scholarly departments. Perhaps this desire for interdisciplinarity is better seen as ill-disciplined. Certainly for its critics, Cultural Studies (and its dispersed effects) has always played fast and loose with the hard-won manners and protocols of professional attention. For such critics, loosening or abandoning disciplinary reins was not just ill-disciplined, but was also the abandonment of scholarly value. For its passionate advocates (and I include myself here, of course) to be ill-disciplined was the requirement of having a sense of living culture in the first place. But did this ill-discipline constitute an abandonment of the sorts of careful attention associated with the disciplines? Did it just junk the long apprenticeships in archival research, literary criticism, anthropological fieldwork, and sociological empiricism for a quick-response (and a superficial one) to the field of culture? Or was its ambition always running ahead of itself, to the point where disciplinary apprenticeships had to be picked up along the way? If so, is there a sense that the practitioner of Cultural Studies is something of an amateur?

Amateurs, though they may lack professional legitimation, are also passionately involved in the knowledges they engage with (the Latin *amator* provides the root of the word amateur: it is the word for a lover). In a world of professionalism and expertise the term has lost its sense of passionate engagement and love of knowledge and has become a word of routine abuse: mess something up and you're labelled an amateur. Amateurs as lovers, though, are not flibbertigibbets, pick-and-mix opinion-mongers, but those who are deeply embroiled in complex worlds of knowledge. Perhaps the ill-disciplined arena of Cultural Studies needs these passionate amateurs, who rather than skimming the surface of the disciplines, saturate themselves as best they can in a number of orientations at once.

In today's scholarly milieu the intellectual past (the time before disciplinary hardening) can seem to be filled with both amateurs and staggeringly ambitious polymaths. You don't have to go back far to get a sense of the broad passions of an era prior to disciplinary hardening: the first Chair of sociology at Birmingham University was given in 1950 to Charles Madge, who was a well-respected published poet; the sociologist, Erving Goffman, was as likely to quote from literature as he was from his ethnographic informants, and as likely to pick up a theoretical point from theatre as from philosophy.

If Cultural Studies starts out from the desire for interdisciplinarity (either implicitly or explicitly) it might do well to cast its net further back than the 1960s. Looking for beginnings (not origins) might take us to places and people who might seem at once both peripheral and central to the passion for Cultural Studies. C. L. R. James, for instance (who we met in chapter three) was a writer whose range included writing history, writing about literature, about politics, about comics and film, about music, and about his abiding love – cricket. As Stuart Hall writes:

> You could say [...] that if your curriculum was to know about the things which James knew about, you would come out of that process knowing about the world, understanding the modern world. You would have taken, eaten, broken bread with the

dramas, with the big things, that have made the modern world. So what do you call someone like that other than world historical, especially if he comes out of Trinidad?

(Hall 1998: 30)

For Hall James is exemplary as an intellectual who is concerned with moments of epochal change, with altering our understanding of modernity, someone who has looked at dramatic events and everyday cultural life. What do you call someone like that? For Hall he is world-historical, but another way of figuring this is to see James as a beginning point for Cultural Studies as an ambitious investigation of passionate culture (a designation that could also be applied to Stuart Hall).

But these messy beginning points could be multiplied. We could also include here the kaleidoscopic work of Walter Benjamin writing in the 1920s and 30s. Benjamin's scope is breathtaking. For someone existing on the very outskirts of the academy (his *habilitation* thesis was rejected by Frankfurt University) he seems to be undaunted by any area of knowledge (philosophy, cultural history, popular culture, and so on). Indeed reading Benjamin you get a sense of what it must be like to not be cowed by specialised expertise. Is there any relationship here between Benjamin's rejection by the academy and his courageous amateurism? Would he have become such a beacon of Cultural Studies' desires if had led a more institutionally scholarly existence?

Zora Neale Hurston studied anthropology with Franz Boas. She never finished her doctoral thesis. But this didn't stop her writing ethnography (of Caribbean religion), folklore studies of African-American culture, as well as novels and plays. Hurston was most active during the 1920s and 1930 when she edited a literary magazine that was central to the Harlem Renaissance and when she was conducting ethnographic research in the Caribbean and in the Southern states of North America. Such crossing of anthropology and literature was not uncommon in these years, but Hurston's ability to vivify the one with the other is exemplary: another possible beginning for Cultural Studies.

Before Art History became obsessed with individual artists and with demarcating artistic schools and visual conundrums it could be seen to have a much larger ambition. The past leaves us many traces of activity, but perhaps the most compelling yet hardest to mobilise are the objects of ordinary life: the plates and vases, the ordinary homes and pieces of decoration left to us by antiquity. For art historians such as Alois Riegl and later Aby Warburg the anonymous history produced by unnamed artisans was as important as the authored works of cathedrals and canonical artworks. Theirs was a concentration that could focus on domesticity and craft (for Riegl this meant looking at belt buckles and rugs) as well as look across epochs and continents. While all of them used images, it is Warburg's *Mnemosyne Atlas* that offers the most striking example of how a display of disparate visual material might build up into a project in its own right. The *Atlas* remained unfinished when he died in 1929 but already in the two years he had been working on it, it contained sixty panels and over one thousand images ranging across painting, photography, architecture, stamps, and so on: artefacts from every time and from every corner of the earth.

Each discipline within the humanities and social sciences has its ill-disciplined impulse that should be remembered and acknowledged by Cultural Studies. These impulses are still present and it is up to present-day practitioners of Cultural Studies to search them out and make common cause with them. We might learn something new from something old. Even if we are interested in the most contemporary phenomena (the ubiquity of mobile phones and the pervasiveness of private life in the public realm, for example) or the most urgent social dilemmas (child labour in East Asia, the collapse of banking systems across the 'first' world) the perspectives provided by C. L. R. James or Zora Neale Hurston, for instance, or by an art history that was always interested in questions of technology offer us a significant beginning for recognising such phenomena.

Where you begin to tell history from; what objects you begin to talk about culture with; whose lives you see culture through – are difficult but central questions for the practice of Cultural Studies. In this book I have been arguing all along that the passions offer a good beginning. So my advice on where to start and what to start with is simple: begin with passion. If you want to start in the midst of things there may be no better place to start than in the tangle of bodies, moods, structures, feelings, manners, and beliefs that constitute passionate culture. Complexity for its own sake of course is worthless. But with the passions you have a way of relating bodies to states of being and states of government; a way of seeing the culture that has got under your skin, into your nervous system and into your gut. A field of passionate study requires a passionate beginning.

Further Reading

To keep this list of further readings to a manageable length I have limited the choice of texts to books and anthologies, and have excluded individual essays and articles. This is not an exhaustive listing of further reading, just a short selection of suggestions.

In this book I have treated cultural studies as an invitation to undertake interdisciplinary work in the study of culture, with a particular eye on what I have been calling passionate culture. In doing so I've had little to say about the disciplinary and institutional forms that have given cultural studies a particular identity and voice over the last fifty years. My advice for people new to Cultural Studies is to worry less about what exactly Cultural Studies is, and to look at what it does (or what it has done, and to imagine what it could do). One place to get a sense of the kind of things that Cultural Studies have puzzled over is in Simon During's *The Cultural Studies Reader*; this large anthology combines theoretical work with passionate engagements with cultural history and experience. Alternatively Lawrence Grossberg, Cary Nelson and Paula Triechler's vast, edited volume simply called *Cultural Studies* provides a snapshot of the ambitiousness and heterogeneity of cultural studies in the 1990s.

For those who do like to know about disciplinary and institutional history Dennis Dworkin's *Cultural Marxism in Postwar Britain: History, the New Left and the Origins of Cultural Studies*, is a detailed account of how Cultural Studies as a scholarly and political project emerged in postwar Britain. Graeme Turner's *British Cultural Studies: an Introduction* is also concerned with the British formation of the enterprise but is organised more thematically. Simon During's recent *Cultural Studies: A Critical Introduction*, while acknowledging the importance of the British tradition of Cultural Studies, is keen to see Cultural Studies within the framework of globalisation, and thus to question what any focus on specific national traditions leaves out of account.

But then again it might serve you best just to launch right in there and start reading a book or two that gets on with studying culture.

For my money a list of the best one hundred cultural studies books of the last twenty-five years would need to include at least these five: Paul Gilroy's *The Black Atlantic*, Kristin Ross' *Fast Cars, Clean Bodies*, Anne McClintock's *Imperial Leather*, Meaghan Morris' *Too Soon Too Late*, and Peter Stallybrass and Allon White's *The Politics and Poetics of Transgression*. Of course as soon as you start singling out specific books and authors a whole host of alternatives spring to mind that would deserve equal prominence as the books I've just mentioned. Perhaps then I should simply say that these five books fired my passion for studying culture and I would hope that they would fire yours too.

This book has mainly stayed within the confines of Britain, North America, South Africa and Australia; the wider world of much of mainland Europe, Russia, China, Japan, Latin America, the Indian subcontinent, Africa, and Asia, is missing. I felt arrogant enough about writing across the wide cultural terrain that I have dealt with here. For a more international version of Cultural Studies I would suggest starting with the anthology *Internationalizing Cultural Studies* edited by Ackbar Abbas and John Nguyet Erni. The literature around globalisation is vast; one good place to start is the anthology *The Cultures of Globalization* edited by Fredric Jameson and Maosao Miyoshi. Working through these two books and pursuing their references will open up something of this larger world.

So far this list of further readings has been concerned with filling some of the gaps that arise when you pose an invitation to participate in the passions of cultural studies. As for further reading that is more directly concerned with the theme of passionate culture and more directly linked to **chapter one** there are a host of books that are concerned with what are variously called passions, emotions, aesthetics and affects. Sue Campbell's *Interpreting the Personal: Expression and the Formation of Feelings* and Sara Ahmed's *The Cultural Politics of Emotion* are both viscerally rich accounts of our passionate life and are clear about why it matters. Philip Fisher's *The Vehement Passions* is philosophically erudite and wonderfully evocative and Richard Meyer's edited anthology *Representing the Passions: Histories, Bodies, Visions*, with its concentration on visual culture is a great way into the topic of passionate culture.

Even if you are not versed in philosophy some of the original texts on the passions are not as difficult to read as may be imagined. David Hume's *A Treatise of Human Nature*, for instance, can be dipped into for what it has to tell us on the passions; and so too can Descartes' *The Passions of the Soul*. A useful guide to the work of Hume is provided by A. J. Ayer's *Hume: A Very Short Introduction*. Michel Meyer's *Philosophy and the Passions: Towards a History of Human Nature*, Robert Solomon's *The Passions: Emotions and the Meaning of Life*, and Thomas Dixon's *From Passions to Emotions: The Creation of a Secular Psychological Category* all embed discussions of the passions in wider philosophical, social and theological debates.

For the work of Gregory Bateson my suggestion would be to start with his *Steps to an Ecology of Mind* and his book on 'naven' ceremonies of the Iatmul people of New Guinea, where he offers the most concrete descriptions of ethos and schismogenesis (the book is called simply *Naven*). It is also worth looking at the work of his contemporary Ruth Benedict and her book *Patterns of Culture*. In lots of ways this was a more influential book than *Naven* and provided one of the references for Raymond Williams' notion of 'structures of feeling' (discussed in chapter three).

For more material on wonder and curiosity, and the passions more generally, as 'royal roads' to knowledge (and the problems that those roads encountered), the best place to begin is with Lorraine Daston and Katharine Park's, *Wonders and the Order of Nature* and Barbara Benedict's *Curiosity: A Cultural History of Early Modern Inquiry*. For a contemporary plea to reinstate wonder as a basis for ethical and political inquiry see Jane Bennett's *The Enchantment of Modern Life: Attachments, Crossings, and Ethics*. An excellent introduction to Cultural Studies and feminism is provided by the anthology *Feminism and Cultural Studies*, edited by Morag Shiach – I can't think of a better place to begin.

Chapter two is concerned with taste: both literally in relation to the sensations of what hits the tongue and the taste buds; and more distantly in the sense of good and bad taste, kitsch taste and aristocratic taste, and so on. The major critique of taste as natural and immutable (beyond historical and cultural contingency) is performed most thoroughly in Pierre Bourdieu's *Distinction: A Social*

Critique of the Judgement of Taste. It is based on ethnographic fieldwork carried out in France in the 1960s. Moving from France to Australia, from the 1960s to the 1990s, Tony Bennett, Michael Emmison and John Frow's *Accounting for Tastes: Australian Everyday Cultures* take up Bourdieu's baton to provide an inventory of taste in a more multicultural society. On the cultural history of taste in relation to styles of behaviour, good manners and etiquette, then the best place to begin is with Norbert Elias' *The Civilizing Process: Sociogenetic and Psychogenetic Investigations*. Penny Sparke's *As Long as its Pink: The Sexual Politics of Taste* concentrates on the gendering of taste, while Elizabeth Guffey's *Retro: The Culture of Revival* looks at the way old tastes return as new cultural enthusiasms.

Writing on food culture is plentiful. For my money I would start with Massimo Montanari's *Food is Culture*, Felipe Fernández-Armesto's *Food: A History* and Margaret Visser's *The Rituals of Dinner: The Origins, Evolution, Eccentricities, and Meaning of Table Manners*. I would follow this with Elspeth Probyn's *Carnal Appetites: FoodSexIdentities*, Jack Goody's *Food and Love* and Wolfgang Schivelbusch *Tastes of Paradise: A Social History of Spices, Stimulants, and Intoxicants*.

The best book on disgust is William Miller's *The Anatomy of Disgust*. For a cultural psychoanalytic approach to disgust and abjection Julia Kristeva's *Powers of Horror: An Essay on Abjection* is the standard work and while it relates abjection to the 'lost mother' it also works to show how abjection is articulated in various forms of racism and xenophobia. For work on shame see Eve Kosofsky Sedgwick, *Touching Feeling: Affect, Pedagogy, Performativity*, Sally Munt's *Queer Attachments: The Cultural Politics of Shame* and Elspeth Probyn, *Blush: Faces of Shame*.

In **chapter three** I aimed to show how passionate culture is distributed unevenly and that this unevenness is both a deep structure but one without predictable outcomes. For an understanding of the passions arising out of colonial encounters and the various political and cultural struggles that have arisen from what is sometimes euphemistically called the 'colonial adventure' the best place to start in my opinion is with Tzvetan Todorov's *The Conquest of America: The Question of the Other*. Paul Gilroy's already mentioned *Black Atlantic* is also crucial. Peter Hulme's *Colonial Encounters: Europe and the Native Caribbean 1492–1797* and Mary Louise Pratt's *Imperial Eyes: Travel Writing and Transculturation* provide inventive theoretical framing for understanding these encounters. For an encyclopaedic and thematic account of anti-colonialism and post-colonialism see Robert Young's *Postcolonialism: An Historical Introduction*. For a useful guide to the way post-colonialism (as an intellectual orientation) is pursued in literary studies see the collection *The Cambridge Companion to Postcolonial Literary Studies* edited by Neil Lazarus.

One of the best ways to get a sense of Raymond Williams' contribution to the study of culture is his book *Marxism and Literature*; here he gives short but vivid accounts of his major preoccupations. I think that his smaller essays have an incisiveness that is compelling and a useful collection of these can be found in *What I came to Say*. The book of interviews *Politics and Letters: Interviews with New Left Review* gives an involved sense of the intellectual context Williams was working within. The best place to start with C. L. R. James is probably his autobiographical book on cricket: *Beyond a Boundary* and to follow this by going to the collection *The C. L. R. James Reader*. Farrukh Dhondy provides a lively biography of James in *C. L. R. James: A Life*.

For a sense of the long histories of black and Asian migration in Britain see Rozina Visram's *Asians in Britain: 400 Years of History* and Peter Fryer's *Staying Power: The History of Black People in Britain*. For a popular account of black and Asian experience in Britain with particular emphasis on London and literature see Sukhdev Sandhu's *London Calling: How Black and Asian Writers Imagined a City*. Susheila Nasta's *Home Truths: Fictions of the South Asian Diaspora in Britain* and James Procter's *Dwelling Places: Postwar Black British Writing* are much more scholarly and both have much to recommend them. For a vivid account of postwar migration in Britain see Mike Phillips and Trevor Phillips' *Windrush: The Irresistible Rise of Multi-Racial Britain*.

In **chapter four** the discussion turned to the world of things; particularly to commercial goods and the passions they animate. To find out more about the culture of World's Fairs and International Exhibitions (Expos, *Expositions Universelles*, etc.) then

Paul Greenhalgh's *Ephemeral Vistas* is a good place to start and takes you from 1851 to 1939, while Andrew Garn's (*et al*) book *Exit to Tomorrow*, a non-academic volume, has great photographs and fills in most of the other years (1933 to 2005). The reference book *Encyclopedia of World's Fairs and Expositions* edited by John Findling and Kimberly Pelle is an indispensable guide to this area of passionate culture, and Anna Jackson's *Expo: International Expositions 1851–2010* is a very good thematic and inclusive account with a useful chronological list of all the world exhibitions. On the Great Exhibition see Jeffrey Auerbach's *The Great Exhibition of 1851: A Nation on Display*, as well as Louise Purbrick's edited collection *The Great Exhibition of 1851: New Interdisciplinary Essays*. Most of the scholarship on World's Fairs is dedicated to the North American experience: see for instance Robert Rydell, *All the World's a Fair* and Robert Rydell, John Findling, and Kimberly Pelle's book *Fair America*, though there are some good books on the French experience (for instance Tag Gronberg's *Designs on Modernity*).

While advertising and promotional culture is often a central component in the teaching of cultural and media studies (as well as design and communication studies) it has not produced a wealth of sparkling literature. Judith Williamson's *Decoding Advertising* which was first published in 1978 is useful but inevitably suffers from her examples seeming quite dated; while W. F. Haug's *Critique of Commodity Aesthetics: Appearance, Sexuality and Advertising in Capitalist Society* benefits from seeing advertising as a whole domain (rather than as specific texts to be decoded for their ideological meanings) it too can now be read historically (it was first published in Germany in 1971). For a useful introduction to the history of advertising and to the practice of studying it, Gillian Dyer's *Advertising as Communication* is a good place to begin. The collection *Buy this Book: Studies in Advertising and Consumption* edited by Andrew Blake, Iain MacRury, Mica Nava and Barry Richards, opened up new avenues of promotional culture some of which have been developed elsewhere. For a lively account of the history of shopping try Laura Byrne Paquet's *The Urge to Splurge: A Social History of Shopping*, or Rachel Bowlby's *Carried Away: The Invention of Modern Shopping*. Reading Elizabeth Wilson's *Adorned in Dreams: Fashion and Modernity* is a great way to get a sense of the importance of fashion for thinking through the passionate experiences of modernity. Christoph Asendorf's *Batteries of Life: On the History of Things and Their Perception in Modernity*, is filled with scintillating examples of the passionate culture of things.

For work on the intimate world of material culture the most vibrant place to begin is Daniel Miller's *The Comfort of Things*. I would follow this by looking at Judy Attfield's *Wild Things* and Louise Purbrick's *The Wedding Present: Domestic Life beyond Consumption*. The book *The Social Life of Things: Commodities in Cultural Perspective* edited by Arjun Appadurai, and Nicholas Thomas' *Entangled Objects: Exchange, Material Culture, and Colonialism in the Pacific* offer a more global perspective on things. Chapter four partly relies on the double sense of possession (as both being in the thrall of something, and intimately owning something) and one place to go for an ambitious working-through of this contrast is Kevin Hetherington's *Capitalism's Eye* which argues that you don't really understand the modern world without recognising the new sorts of subjectivity that commodity culture introduced. This book also offers a useful introduction to the work of Walter Benjamin, but if you wanted more of an introduction to Benjamin then Peter Buse, Ken Hirschkop, Scott McCracken and Bertrand Taithe's *Benjamin's Arcades: An unguided Tour* is a great place to start. There is a mass of secondary writing on Benjamin, but the primary texts are very easy to get hold of and usually make for exhilarating reading.

In **chapter five** I looked at communication media (if that isn't a tautology) as passionate culture. I focused specifically on photography, sound recording and broadcast media (TV and radio). For a foundational history of media the best place to start is Asa Briggs' and Peter Burke's *A Social History of the Media: From Gutenberg to the Internet*. Paddy Scannell's *Radio, Television and Modern Life* and Roger Silverstone's *Television and Everyday Life* are not introductory volumes but in their different ways they are fascinating attempts to understand media as passionate experiential culture. For an earlier attempt at this see Raymond Williams' *Television: Technology and Cultural Form*.

The best introduction to photography is, I think, Steve Edwards' book *Photography: A Very Short Introduction*. But if you want a direct 'hit' of photography as passionate culture you might watch two films that cast Timothy Spall as intimately entangled with photography: in Stephen Poliakoff's *Shooting the Past*, Spall plays an intransigent photographic librarian who has an amazing ability to trace specific people across an enormous archive of images; in Mike Leigh's *Secrets and Lies*, he plays a photographer ensnared in a family drama animated by envy and misunderstandings. In both instances the world of photographic images takes us beyond the confines of the immediate difficulty and out into a world of other struggles, other difficulties.

The idea that media forms are often haunted by otherworldly desires (death, fairies, spirit communication, and so on) is the topic of a number of books. John Durham Peter's *Speaking into the Air: A History of the Idea of Communication*, is a detailed philosophical book that shows how the failure of communication is a constituent aspect of all communication. Jeffrey Sconce's *Haunted Media: Electronic Presence from Telegraphy to Television* is also useful here. For a more general account of the ghostly as a category for thinking about the social then Avery Gordon's *Ghostly Matters: Haunting and the Sociological Imagination* is particularly useful.

For an account of the early years of the telephone in North America see Claude Fisher's *America Calling: A Social History of the Telephone to 1940*. The collection *The Social Impact of the Telephone*, edited by Ithiel de Sola Pool is essential reading. On mobile phone culture (or cell phone culture) see Gerard Goggin's *Cell Phone Culture: Mobile Technology in Everyday Life*; this book also has a substantial bibliography of texts relating to its topic. For me the best book on the history of audio culture is Jonathan Sterne's *The Audible Past: Cultural Origins of Sound Reproduction*. For more information and commentary on the wonderful artwork of Susan Hiller see *Susan Hiller: Recall – Selected Works 1969–2004*, edited by James Lingwood.

In **chapter six**, the last substantive chapter, we end up, as is only proper, in the throes of love, but also, as might sometimes seem inevitable, in the thrall of loss and hurt. Stephen Kern's *The Culture of Love: Victorians to Moderns* and Ole Høystad's *A History of the Heart* provide a foundation in the cultural history of love and loss. The last three volumes of the massive five-volume *A History* *of Private Life* (written under the general editorship of Philippe Ariès and Georges Duby) are also extremely useful on the vicissitudes of emotional manners.

The problem of conceptualising and mobilising 'experience' as a category for the study of culture (in practical and theoretical work) is historically explored in Martin Jay's *Songs of Experience: Modern American and European Variations on a Universal Theme*. Jay, as always, is a trustworthy guide through the thickets of intellectual debate. Michael Pickering's *History, Experience and Cultural Studies* and Graig Ireland's *The Subaltern Appeal to Experience: Self-Identity, Late Modernity, and the Politics of Immediacy* are also valuable (the former offers a more introductory guide to the knotty realm of experience than the latter).

Work on deconstruction and performativity are only really touched on here. In an earlier book (*Michel de Certeau: Analysing Culture*) I focus on the possibilities for reading and listening that an involvement with poststructuralist doubt can open-up rather than close-down. My position is that the kinds of scepticism foregrounded by the work of Derrida and others (the work of Michel de Certeau is, I argue, central here), establishes the possibilities, opportunities and responsibilities for hearing and registering the passionate life of others (however incomplete and speculative this registering might be). Work by and on Derrida is extensive. A short introduction to his early work is provided by Christopher Norris in *Deconstruction: Theory and Practice* and the anthology *Derrida: A Critical Reader*, edited by David Wood offers a number of useful essays. Catherine Belsey's *Critical Practice* is a worthwhile introduction to the field of poststructuralist thought.

The idea of attending to the performativity of culture (rather than its representational adequacy), which is only implicit here, is developed in a number of places, most notably in the work of Judith Butler but also in performance studies more generally. Judith Butler's *Gender Trouble: Feminism and the Subversion of Identity* and her *Bodies that Matter: On the Discursive Limits of Sex* are the obvious places to begin. For her more recent work see, for example, *Precarious Life: The Power of Mourning and Violence*. For an inspired account of pursuing the performative in art and performance art in particular see Peggy Phelan's *Unmarked: The Politics of Performance*.

The terrible plight of the Stolen Generations is detailed in *Bringing them Home: The Report of the National Inquiry into the Separation of Aboriginal and Torres Strait Islander Children from Their Families* and can be accessed in full at: http://www.austlii.edu.au/au/special/ rsjproject/rsjlibrary/hreoc/stolen/. It does not make for easy reading. There are a number of projects collecting oral histories which can be found on the internet by searching 'stolen generations'. Both Sara Ahmed (in *The Cultural Politics of Emotion*) and Elspeth Probyn (in *Blush: Faces of Shame*) write about the forced removals of aboriginal and Torres Strait Islander children. Peter Read's *A Rape of the Soul so Profound: The Return of the Stolen Generation* and Linda Biskman's *The Black Grapevine: Aboriginal Activism and the Stolen Generation* offer very different accounts of the forced removals.

Chapter seven is an invitation to think about method and approach by suggesting that there are always numerous places to begin, and that beginning in one place rather than another has consequences. It would seem against the spirit of that chapter to then give you a list of books telling you what to begin thinking about and where to begin. However here I do want to just point in the direction of a few significant books and starting places that pursue some of the frames suggested here.

For thinking of the modern as a mid nineteenth century affair I've found T. J. Clark's *The Painting of Modern Life: Paris in the Art of Manet and his Followers* to be a fascinating account told through the strange surfaces and arrangements of Manet's paintings. Lynda Nead's *Victorian Babylon: People, Streets and Images in Nineteenth-Century London* is also essential. For a general introduction to modernity and the passion of the modern you can't beat John Jervis' *Exploring the Modern*. For the modern as it is imagined at the turn of the nineteenth into the twentieth century Leo Charney and Vanessa Schwartz's edited collection *Cinema and the Invention of Modern Life* is full of fascinating material. Terry Smith's *Making the Modern: Industry, Art, and Design in America* is a fulsome account of the modern in the early decades of the twentieth century.

For a sense of the eighteenth century modern I would suggest Miles Ogborn's *Spaces of Modernity: London's Geographies 1680–1780*, and Terry Castle's *The Female Thermometer: Eighteenth-Century Culture and the Invention of the Uncanny*: both fascinating investigations of an earlier modern. An account of how you might see the modern in the early decades of the nineteenth century Jane Rendell's *The Pursuit of Pleasure: Gender, Space and Architecture in Regency London* is very good. For accounts of the modern that aren't oriented to Europe and America one good place to start is the collection, *Becoming Chinese: Passages to Modernity and Beyond*, edited by Wen-Hsin Yeh and the collection *Modernity and Culture: From the Mediterranean to the Indian Ocean* edited by Leila Tarazi Fawaz and C. A. Byly. Another single year book to add to the list (but there must be hundreds more) is Jonathan Schneer's *London 1900: The Imperial Metropolis*. For more on the work of Riegl and Warburg see the two collections edited by Richard Woodfield *Art History as Cultural History: Warburg's Projects* and *Framing Formalism: Riegl's Work*.

Bibliography

Abbas, Ackbar and John Nguyet Erni eds (2005) *Internationalizing Cultural Studies: An Anthology*, Oxford: Blackwell.

Ahmed, Sara (2004) *The Cultural Politics of Emotion*, Edinburgh: Edinburgh University Press.

Altieri, Charles (2003) *The Particulars of Rapture: An Aesthetics of the Affects*, Ithaca: Cornell University Press.

Andriopoulos, Stefan (2005) 'Psychic Television', *Critical Inquiry*, 31, pp. 618–37.

Appadurai, Arjun ed. (1986) *The Social Life of Things: Commodities in Cultural Perspective*, Cambridge: Cambridge University Press.

Ardis, Ann L. and Leslie W. Lewis eds (2003) *Women's Experience of Modernity 1875–1945*, Baltimore and London: Johns Hopkins University Press.

Ariès, Philippe and Georges Duby, general editors (1989) *A History of Private Life, Volume 3: Passions of the Renaissance*, edited by Roger Chartier, translated by Arthur Goldhammer, Cambridge, Mass.: Belknap Press.

—— (1990) *A History of Private Life, Volume 4: From the Fires of Revolution to the Great War*, edited by Michelle Perrot, translated by Arthur Goldhammer, Cambridge, Mass.: Belknap Press.

—— (1991) *A History of Private Life, Volume 5: Riddles of Identity in Modern Times*, edited by Antoine Prost and Gérard Vincent, translated by Arthur Goldhammer, Cambridge, Mass.: Belknap Press.

Asendorf, Christoph (1993) *Batteries of Life: On the History of Things and Their Perception in Modernity*, translated by Don Reneau, Berkeley, Los Angeles, and London: University of California Press.

Attfield, Judy (2000) *Wild Things: The Material Culture of Everyday Life*, Oxford and New York: Berg.

Attwood, Janet Bray and Chris Attwood (2007) *The Passion Test: The Effortless Path to Discovering Your Destiny*, London: Simon & Schuster.

Auerbach, Jeffrey A. (1999) *The Great Exhibition of 1851: A Nation on Display*, New Haven and London: Yale University Press.

Austin, J. L. (1989 [1962]) *How to do Things with Words*, Oxford: Oxford University Press.

Ayer, A. J. (2000 [1980]) *Hume: A Very Short Introduction*, Oxford: Oxford University Press.

Barthes, Roland (1979 [1977]) *A Lover's Discourse: Fragments*, translated by Richard Howard, London: Jonathan Cape.

—— (1984 [1980]) *Camera Lucida: Reflections on Photography*, translated by Richard Howard, London: Fontana.

Batchen, Geoffrey (2004) *Forget Me Not: Photography & Remembrance*, New York: Princeton Architectural Press.

Bateson, Gregory (1935) 'Culture, Contact and Schismogenesis', *Man*, December, item 199, pp. 178–183.

—— (1958 [1936]) *Naven* (second edition), Stanford: Stanford University Press.

—— (1972) *Steps to an Ecology of Mind*, Chicago: University of Chicago Press.

Battersby, Christine (1989) *Gender and Genius: Towards a Feminist Aesthetics*, London: Women's Press.

Beller, Miles (2000) *Dream of Venus (or Living Pictures)*, Beverly Hills, California: C. M. Publishing.

Belsey, Catherine (1980) *Critical Practice*, London: Methuen.

Benedict, Burton (1983) *The Anthropology of World's Fairs: San Francisco's Panama Pacific International Exposition of 1915* (with contributions by Marjorie M. Dobkin, Gray Brechin, Elizabeth N. Armstrong and George Starr), London and Berkeley: Scolar Press.

Benedict, Barbara M. (2002) *Curiosity: A Cultural History of Early Modern Inquiry*, Chicago: University of Chicago Press.

Benedict, Ruth (1934) *Patterns of Culture*, Boston: Houghton Mifflin Company.

Benjamin, Walter (1934) 'The Author as Producer', in *Understanding Brecht*, translated by Anna Bostock, London: Verso, 1983, pp. 85–103.

—— (1999) *The Arcades Project*, translated by Howard Eiland and Kevin McLaughlin, Cambridge, Mass. and London: Harvard University Press.

Bennett, Jane (2001) *The Enchantment of Modern Life: Attachments, Crossings, and Ethics*, Princeton: Princeton University Press.

Bennett, Tony, Michael Emmison and John Frow (1999) *Accounting for Tastes: Australian Everyday Cultures*, Cambridge: Cambridge University Press.

Biskman, Linda (2003) *The Black Grapevine: Aboriginal Activism and the Stolen Generation*, Annandale, NSW: Federation Press.

Blake, Andrew *et al* (1996) *Buy This Book: Studies in Advertising and Consumption*, London and New York: Routledge.

Bourdieu, Pierre (1977) *Outline of a Theory of Practice*, translated by Richard Nice, Cambridge: Cambridge University Press.

—— (1992 [1979]) *Distinction: A Social Critique of the Judgement of Taste*, London: Routledge.

Bowlby, Rachel (2000) *Carried Away: The Invention of Modern Shopping*, London: Faber and Faber.

Briggs, Asa and Peter Burke (2002) *A Social History of the Media: From Gutenberg to the Internet*, Cambridge: Polity.

Buse, Peter *et al* (2005) *Benjamin's Arcades: An Unguided Tour*, Manchester: Manchester University Press.

Butler, Judith (1990) *Gender Trouble: Feminism and the Subversion of Identity*, New York and London: Routledge.

—— (1993) *Bodies that Matter: On the Discursive Limits of Sex*, New York and London: Routledge.

—— (2006) *Precarious Life: The Power of Mourning and Violence*, London: Verso.

Campbell, Sue (1997) *Interpreting the Personal: Expression and the Formation of Feelings*, Ithaca and London: Cornell University Press.

Castle, Terry (1995) *The Female Thermometer: Eighteenth-Century Culture and the Invention of the Uncanny*, New York and Oxford, Oxford University Press.

Chakrabarty, Dipesh (2002) 'Museums in Late Democracies', *Humanities Research*, 9, 1, pp. 5–12.

Charney, Leo and Vanessa R. Schwartz eds (1996) *Cinema and the Invention of Modern Life*, Berkeley: University of California Press.

Clark, T. J. (1985) *The Painting of Modern Life: Paris in the Art of Manet and his Followers*, London: Thames and Hudson.

Colomina, Beatriz (2001) 'Enclosed by Images: The Eameses' Multimedia Architecture', *Grey Room*, 2, pp. 6–29.

Connor, Steven (2003) 'Not All of One Mind: Psychoanalysis and Cultural-analysis', http://www.bbk.ac.uk/english/skc/onemind/, last accessed 9 October 2008.

Coombes, Annie E. (2003) *Visual Culture and Public Memory in a Democratic South Africa*, Durham NC: Duke University Press.

Crary, Jonathan (1997) 'Spectacle, Attention, Counter-Memory', in *October: The Second Decade, 1986–1996*, edited by Rosalind Krauss, *et al*, Cambridge, Mass. and London: MIT Press, pp. 415–425.

Darwin, Charles (1999 [1872]) *The Expression of the Emotions in Man and Animals* (third edition), London: Fontana Press [first edition published in 1872, second 1889].

Daston, Lorraine and Katharine Park (2001) *Wonders and the Order of Nature*, New York: Zone Books.

de Certeau, Michel (1984) *The Practice of Everyday Life*, translated by Steven Rendall, Berkeley: University of California Press.

Derrida, Jacques (1971) 'Signature, Event, Context', in *Margins of Philosophy*, translated by Alan Bass, Brighton: Harvester, pp. 309–330.

—— (1988) *Limited Inc*, Evanston, Il.: Northwestern University Press.

Descartes, René (1989 [1649]) *The Passions of the Soul*, translated by Stephen H. Voss, Indianapolis and Cambridge: Hackett.

Dhondy, Farrukh (2001) *C. L. R. James: A Life*, New York: Pantheon Books.

Dixon, Thomas (2003) *From Passions to Emotions: The Creation of a Secular Psychological Category*, Cambridge: Cambridge University Press.

Docker, John (2001) *1492: The Poetics of Diaspora*, London and New York: Continuum.

Doctorow, E. L. (1985) *World's Fair*, London: Picador.

During, Simon (2005) *Cultural Studies: A Critical Introduction*, Abingdon and New York: Routledge.

During, Simon ed. (1999) *The Cultural Studies Reader*, London and New York: Routledge.

Dworkin, Dennis (1997) *Cultural Marxism in Postwar Britain: History, the New Left and the Origins of Cultural Studies*, Durham N.C. and London: Duke University Press.

Dyer, Gillian (1982) *Advertising as Communication*, London: Methuen.

Eagleton, Terry (1990) *The Ideology of the Aesthetic*, Oxford: Blackwell.

Edwards, Steve (2006) *Photography: A Very Short Introduction*, Oxford: Oxford University Press.

Elias, Norbert (2000 [1936]) *The Civilizing Process: Sociogenetic and Psychogenetic Investigations*, translated by Edmund Jephcott, Oxford: Blackwell.

Fawaz, Leila Tarazi and C. A. Bayly (2002) *Modernity and Culture from the Mediterranean to the Indian Ocean, 1890–1920*, New York: Columbia University Press.

Fernández-Armesto, Felipe (2002) *Food: A History*, London: Pan.

Findling, John E. and Kimberly D. Pelle, eds (2008) *Encyclopedia of World's Fairs and Expositions*, Jefferson, N.C.: McFarland.

Fisher, Claude S. (1994) *America Calling: A Social History of the Telephone to 1940*, Berkeley: University of California Press.

Fisher, Philip (2002) *The Vehement Passions*, Princeton: Princeton University Press.

Flusser, Vilém (2002) *Writings*, translated by Erik Eisel, edited by Andreas Ströhl, Minneapolis: University of Minnesota Press.

Fortune, Linda (1996) *The House in Tyne Street: Childhood Memories of District Six*, Cape Town: Kwela Books.

Franzen, Jonathan (2001) *The Corrections*, London: HarperCollins.

Fryer, Peter (1984) *Staying Power: The History of Black People in Britain*, London: Pluto.

Garn, Andrew *et al* (2007) *Exit to Tomorrow: History of the Future, World's Fair Architecture, Design, Fashion 1933–2005*, New York: Universe.

Geertz, Clifford (1993) *Local Knowledge: Further Essays in Interpretative Anthropology*, London: Fontana.

Gigante, Denise (2005) *Taste: A Literary History*, New Haven and London: Yale University Press.

Gilroy, Paul (1993) *The Black Atlantic: Modernity and Double Consciousness*, London and New York: Verso.

Goody, Jack (1998) *Food and Love*, London: Verso.

Goggin, Gerard (2006) *Cell Phone Culture: Mobile Technology in Everyday Life*, Abingdon: Routledge.

Gordon, Avery F. (2008 [1997]) *Ghostly Matters: Haunting and the Sociological Imagination*, Minneapolis: University of Minnesota Press.

Greenhalgh, Paul (1988) *Ephemeral Vistas: The Expositions Universelles, Great Exhibitions and World's Fairs, 1851–1939*, Manchester: Manchester University Press.

Gronberg, Tag (1998) *Designs on Modernity: Exhibiting the City in 1920s Paris*, Manchester: Manchester University Press.

Gronow, Jukka (1997) *The Sociology of Taste*, London and New York: Routledge.

Guffey, Elizabeth E. (2006) *Retro: The Culture of Revival*, London: Reaktion Books.

Gumbrecht, Hans Ulrich (1997) *In 1926: Living at the Edge of Time*, Cambridge Mass.: Harvard University Press.

Hall, Stuart (1987) 'Minimal Selves' in *Identity: The Real Me* edited by Lisa Apiganesi, London: ICA Documents, pp. 44–47.

Hall, Stuart (interviewed by Bill Schwarz) (1998) 'Breaking Bread with History: C. L. R. James and *The Black Jacobins*', *History Workshop Journal*, 46, pp. 17–31.

Harrison, Helen A. (1980) 'The Fair Perceived: Color and Light as Elements in Design and Planning', in *Dawn of a New Day: The New York World's Fair, 1939/40*, edited by Helen A. Harrison, New York and London: New York University Press, pp. 43–55.

Haug, W. F. (1986 [1971]) *Critique of Commodity Aesthetics: Appearance, Sexuality and Advertising in Capitalist Society*, Oxford: Blackwell.

Hetherington, Kevin (2007) *Capitalism's Eye: Cultural Spaces of the Commodity*, London and New York: Routledge.

Highmore, Ben (2001) 'Well-upholstered', in *Things*, 14, pp. 98–100.

—— (2006) *Michel de Certeau: Analysing Culture*, London and New York: Continuum.

Hiller, Susan (1986) *Susan Hiller* (exhibition catalogue), London: ICA.

Hirschman, Albert O. (1997 [1977]) *The Passions and the Interests: Political Arguments for Capitalism before its Triumph*, Princeton, NJ: Princeton University Press.

Ho, Elaine Yee Lin (2000) *Timothy Mo*, Manchester: Manchester University Press.

Hooker, Edward (1934) 'The Discussion of Taste, from 1750–1770, and the New Trends in Literary Criticism', *PMLA*, 49, 2, pp. 577–592.

Høystad, Ole M. (2007) *A History of the Heart*, London: Reaktion books.

Hulme, Peter (1986) *Colonial Encounters: Europe and the Native Caribbean 1492–1797*, London and New York: Routledge.

Human Rights and Equal Opportunity Commission (1997) *Bringing Them Home: The Report of the National Inquiry into the Separation of Aboriginal and Torres Strait Islander Children from Their Families*, Commonwealth of Australia, accessed at: http://www.austlii.edu.au/au/special/rsjproject/rsjlibrary/hreoc/stolen/ Last accessed 15 October 2008.

Hume, David (1985 [1739–40]) *A Treatise of Human Nature*, London: Penguin.

—— (1757) 'Of the Standard of Taste', *Selected Essays*, Oxford: Oxford University Press, 1998, pp. 133–154.

Hurston, Zora Neale (1990 [1935]) *Mules and Men*, New York: Harper-Collins.

—— (1990 [1938]) *Tell My Horse: Voodoo and Life in Haiti and Jamaica*, New York: HarperCollins.

Jackson, Anna (2008) *Expo: International Expositions 1851–2010*, London: V&A Publishing.

James, C. L. R. (1962) 'From Toussaint L'Ouverture to Fidel Castro', in *The C. L. R. James Reader*, edited by Anna Grimshaw, Oxford: Blackwell, 1992, pp. 296–314.

—— (1963) *Beyond a Boundary*, London: Hutchinson.

—— (1992) *The C. L. R. James Reader*, edited by Anna Grimshaw, Oxford: Blackwell.

—— (1993) *American Civilization*, Oxford: Blackwell.

—— (2001 [1938]) *The Black Jacobins: Toussaint L'Ouverture and the San Domingo Revolution*, London: Penguin Books.

James, William (1884) 'What is an Emotion?', *Mind*, 9, 34, pp. 188–205.

Jameson, Fredric and Masao Miyoshi eds (1998) *The Cultures of Globalization*, Durham: Duke University Press.

Jay, Martin (2005) *Songs of Experience: Modern American and European Variations on a Universal Theme*, Berkeley: University of California Press.

Jennings, Humphrey (1995) *Pandæmonium: The Coming of the Machine As Seen by Contemporary Observers*, Basingstoke: Macmillan.

Katz, Jack (1999) *How Emotions Work*, Chicago: University of Chicago Press.

Kern, Stephen (1992) *The Culture of Love: Victorians to Moderns*, Cambridge, Mass.: Harvard University Press.

Kirkham, Pat (1995) *Charles and Ray Eames: Designers of the Twentieth Century*, Cambridge and London: MIT Press.

Kristeva, Julia (1982) *Powers of Horror: An Essay on Abjection*, translated by Leon S. Roudiez, New York: Columbia University Press.

—— (1989) *Black Sun: Depression and Melancholia*, translated by Leon S. Roudiez, New York: Columbia University Press.

—— (1996) *Interviews*, edited by Ross Mitchell Guberman, New York: Columbia University Press.

Lazarus, Neil ed. (2004) *The Cambridge Companion to Postcolonial Literary Studies*, Cambridge: Cambridge University Press.

Lefebvre, Henri (1984 [1968]) *Everyday Life in the Modern World* translated by Sacha Rabinovitch, New Brunswick: Transaction Publishers.

Lerner, Arnold (1963) 'IBM press release', April 18, non-paginated.

Linebaugh, Peter and Marcus Rediker (2000) *The Many-Headed Hydra: The Hidden History of the Revolutionary Atlantic*, London: Verso.

Lingwood, James ed. (2004) *Susan Hiller: Recall – Selected Works 1969–2004*, Gateshead: Baltic.

Lutz, Tom (2001) *Crying: The Natural and Cultural History of Tears*, New York and London: Norton.

Lynes, Russell (1954) *The Tastemakers*, New York: Harper.

McClintock, Anne (1995) *Imperial Leather: Race, Gender and Sexuality in the Colonial Contest*, London and New York: Routledge.

McEachern, Charmaine (1998) 'Mapping the Memories: Politics, Place and Identity in District Six Museum, Cape Town', *Social Identities*, 4, 3, pp. 499–521.

Maart, Rozena (2004) *Rosa's District 6*, Ontario: TSAR.

Manganaro, Marc (2002) *Culture, 1922: The Emergence of a Concept*, Princeton: Princeton University Press.

Marcus, Laura (2007) *The Tenth Muse: Writing about Cinema in the Modernist Period*, Oxford: Oxford University Press.

Marx, Karl (1976 [1867]) *Capital: Volume 1*, translated by Ben Fowkes, Harmondsworth: Penguin.

Meyer, Michel (2000) *Philosophy and the Passions: Towards a History of Human Nature*, translated by Robert F. Barsky, University Park Pennsylvania: Pennsylvania State University Press.

Meyer, Richard ed. (2003) *Representing the Passions: Histories, Bodies, Visions*, Los Angeles: Getty Publications.

Miller, Daniel (2008) *The Comfort of Things*, Cambridge: Polity.

Miller, William Ian (1997) *The Anatomy of Disgust*, Cambridge, Mass.: Harvard University Press.

Mo, Timothy (2003 [1982]) *Sour Sweet*, London: Paddleless.

Montanari, Massimo (2006) *Food is Culture*, translated by Albert Sonnenfeld, New York: Columbia University Press.

Munt, Sally R (2007) *Queer Attachments: The Cultural Politics of Shame*, Aldershot: Ashgate.

Nasta, Susheila (2002) *Home Truths: Fictions of the South Asian Diaspora in Britain*, Basingstoke: Palgrave.

Nead, Lynda (2000) *Victorian Babylon: People, Streets and Images in Nineteenth-Century London*, New Haven and London: Yale University Press.

Ngai, Sianne (2005) *Ugly Feelings*, Cambridge, Mass.: Harvard University Press.

—— (2008) 'Merely Interesting', *Critical Inquiry*, 34, 4, pp. 777–817.

Ngcelwane, Nomvuyo (1998) *Sala Kahle District Six: An African Woman's Perspective*, Cape Town: Kwela.

North, Michael (1999) *Reading 1922: A Return to the Scene of the Modern*, New York: Oxford University Press.

Ogborn, Miles (1998) *Spaces of Modernity: London's Geographies 1680–1780*, London: Guilford Press.

Olalquiaga, Celeste (1999) *The Artificial Kingdom: A Treasury of the Kitsch Experience*, London: Bloomsbury.

Orwell, George (1947) 'Such, Such Were the Joys', in, *Collected Essays, Journalism and Letters: In Front of Your Nose, 1945–50*, Harmondsworth: Penguin, 1980, pp. 379–422.

—— (1975 [1937]) *The Road to Wigan Pier*, London: Penguin.

—— (2003 [1933]) *Down and Out in Paris and London*, London: Penguin.

Paquet, Laura Byrne (2003) *The Urge to Splurge: A Social History of Shopping*, Toronto: ECW Press.

Parry, Benita (2004) *Postcolonial Studies: A Materialist Critique*, London and New York: Routledge.

Peters, John Durham N.C. (1999) *Speaking into the Air: A History of the Idea of Communication*, Chicago: University of Chicago Press.

Peterson, Richard A. and Roger M. Kern (1996) 'Changing Highbrow: From Snob to Omnivore', *American Sociological Review*, 16, 5, pp. 900–907.

Phelan, Peggy (1993) *Unmarked: The Politics of Performance*, London and New York: Routledge.

Phillips, Mike (2001) *London Crossings: A Biography of Black Britain*, London and New York: Continuum.

Phillips, Mike and Trevor Phillips (1999) *Windrush: The Irresistible Rise of Multi-Racial Britain*, London: HarperCollins.

Pickering, Michael (1997) *History, Experience and Cultural Studies*, Basingstoke: Macmillan.

Pilkington-Garimara, Doris (1996) *Rabbit-Proof Fence*, New York: Miramax Books.

Plath, Sylvia (2001[1963]) *The Bell Jar*, London: Faber and Faber.

Pickering, Michael (1997) *History, Experience and Cultural Studies*, Basingstoke: Macmillan Press.

Poliakoff, Stephen (1998) *Shooting the Past*, London: Methuen.

Pool, Ithiel de Sola ed. (1977) *The Social Impact of the Telephone*, Cambridge, Mass.: MIT Press.

Porter, Roy (2001) *Enlightenment: Britain and the Creation of the Modern World*, London: Penguin Books.

—— (2004) *Flesh in the Age of Reason*, London: Penguin Books.

Pratt, Mary Louise (1992) *Imperial Eyes: Travel Writing and Transculturation*, London and New York: Routledge.

Probyn, Elspeth (2000) *Carnal Appetites: FoodSexIdentities*, London and New York: Routledge.

—— (2005) *Blush: Faces of Shame*, Minneapolis: University of Minnesota Press.

Procter, James (2003) *Dwelling Places: Postwar Black British Writing*, Manchester: Manchester University Press.

Purbrick, Louise (2007) *The Wedding Present: Domestic Life beyond Consumption*, Aldershot: Ashgate.

Purbrick, Louise ed. (2001) *The Great Exhibition of 1851: New Interdisciplinary Essays*, Manchester: Manchester University Press.

Rakow, Lana F. (1988) 'Women and the Telephone: The Gendering of a Communication Technology', in *Technology and Women's Voices: Keeping in Touch*, edited by Cheris Kramarae, New York and London: Routledge & Kegan Paul, pp. 207–228.

Rancière, Jacques (2004) *The Politics of Aesthetics: The Distribution of the Sensible*, translated by Gabriel Rockhill, London and New York: Continuum.

Ramsay, Gordon (1996) *Gordon Ramsay's Passion for Flavour*, London: Conran Octopus.

Read, Peter (1999) *A Rape of the Soul so Profound: The Return of the Stolen Generation*, Sydney: Allen & Unwin.

Rendell, Jane (2002) *The Pursuit of Pleasure: Gender, Space and Architecture in Regency London*, London: Athlone Press.

Rhys, Jean (1934) *Voyage in the Dark*, London: Constable & Co.

Rive, Richard (1987) *Buckingham Palace, District Six*, London: Heinemann.

Ross, Kristin (1995) *Fast Cars, Clean Bodies: Decolonization and the Reordering of French Culture*, Cambridge, Mass.: MIT Press.

Rydell, Robert W. (1984) *All the World's a Fair*, Chicago: University of Chicago Press.

Rydell, Robert W. John E. Findling, and Kimberly D. Pelle (2000) *Fair America: World's Fairs in the United States*, Washington: Smithsonian Institution.

Said, Edward W. (1985 [1975]) *Beginnings: Intention and Method*, New York: Columbia University Press.

Sanborn, Mark (2004) *The Fred Factor (How passion in your work and life can turn the ordinary into the extraordinary)*, London: Random House.

Sandhu, Sukhdev (2004) *London Calling: How Black and Asian Writers Imagined a City*, London: HarperCollins.

Scannell, Paddy (1996) *Radio, Television and Modern Life*, Oxford: Blackwell.

Shiach, Morag ed. (1999) *Feminism and Cultural Studies*, Oxford: Oxford University Press.

Schivelbusch, Wolfgang (1993) *Tastes of Paradise: A Social History of Spices, Stimulants, and Intoxicants*, translated by David Jacobson, New York: Vintage Books.

Schwartz, Vanessa R. (1998) *Spectacular Realities: Early Mass Culture in Fin-de-Siècle Paris*, Berkeley, Los Angeles, and London: University of California Press.

Schneer, Jonathan (1999) *London 1900: The Imperial Metropolis*, New Haven and London: Yale University Press.

Sconce, Jeffrey (2000) *Haunted Media: Electronic Presence from Telegraphy to Television*, Durham N.C.: Duke University Press.

Scully, Vincent Jr. (1964) 'If This Is Architecture, God Help Us', *Life* 57, July 31, p. 9.

Sedgwick, Eve Kosofsky (2003) *Touching Feeling: Affect, Pedagogy, Performativity*, Durham N.C.: Duke University Press.

Selvon, Sam (2006 [1956]) *The Lonely Londoners*, London: Penguin.

—— (1979) 'Three Into One Can't Go – East Indian, Trinidadian, Westindian', in *India in the Caribbean*, edited by David Dabydeen and Brinsley Samaroo, London: Hansib, 1987, pp. 13–24.

Silverstone, Roger (1994) *Television and Everyday Life*, London and New York: Routledge.

Smith, Terry (1993) *Making the Modern: Industry, Art, and Design in America*, Chicago: University of Chicago Press.

Solomon, Robert C. (1993 [1976]) *The Passions: Emotions and the Meaning of Life*, Indianapolis: Hackett Publishing.

—— (2003) *Not Passion's Slave: Emotions and Choice*, Oxford: Oxford University Press.

Sparke, Penny (1995) *As Long as its Pink: The Sexual Politics of Taste*, London: Harper Collins.

Stallybrass, Peter and White, Allon (1986) *The Politics and Poetics of Transgression*, Ithaca: Cornell University Press.

Sterne, Jonathan (2003) *The Audible Past: Cultural Origins of Sound Reproduction*, Durham N.C. and London: Duke University Press.

Thomas, Nicholas (1991) *Entangled Objects: Exchange, Material Culture, and Colonialism in the Pacific*, Cambridge, Mass. and London: Harvard University Press.

Todorov, Tzvetan (1999 [1982]) *The Conquest of America: The Question of the Other*, translated by Richard Howard, Norman: University of Oklahoma Press.

Turner, Graeme (1992) *British Cultural Studies: An Introduction*, London: Routledge.

Visram, Rozina (2002) *Asians in Britain: 400 Years of History*, London: Pluto Press.

Visser, Margaret (1992) *The Rituals of Dinner: The Origins, Evolution, Eccentricities, and Meaning of Table Manners*, New York and London: Penguin.

Williams, Raymond (1977) *Marxism and Literature*, Oxford: Oxford University Press.

—— (1981) *Politics and Letters: Interviews with New Left Review*, London: Verso.

—— (1989) *What I Came to Say*, London: Hutchinson Radius.

—— (1990 [1975]) *Television: Technology and Cultural Form*, edited by Ederyn Williams, London: Routledge.

—— (1992 [1961]) *The Long Revolution*, London: Hogarth Press.

Williams, Raymond and Michael Orrom (1954) *Preface to Film*, London: Film Drama.

Williamson, Judith (1978) *Decoding Advertisements: Ideology and Meaning in Advertising*, London: Marion Boyars.

Wilson, Elizabeth (2000) *Adorned in Dreams: Fashion and Modernity*, London: Virago.

Woodfield, Richard ed. (2001a) *Art History as Cultural History: Warburg's Projects*, Amsterdam: G + B Arts.

Woodfield, Richard ed. (2001b) *Framing Formalism: Riegl's Work*, Amsterdam: G + B Arts.

Wypijewski, JoAnn ed. (1999) *Painting by Numbers: Komar and Melamid's Scientific Guide to Art*, Berkeley: University of California.

Yeh, Wen-hsin ed. (2000) *Becoming Chinese: Passages to Modernity and Beyond*, Berkeley: University of California Press.

Young, Robert (2001) *Postcolonialism: An Historical Introduction*, Oxford: Blackwell.

Index